*A Project Test Pattern Book
in Parish Development*

NEW HOPE
FOR
CONGREGATIONS

Loren B. Mead
with research assistance of
Elisa L. DesPortes

Foreword by Reuel L. Howe

A Crossroad Book

THE SEABURY PRESS • NEW YORK

New Hope for Congregations is published under the auspices of the National Advisory Committee on Evangelism, the Rt. Rev. Lloyd Gressle, Chairman, and the Executive Council of the Episcopal Church.

Copyright © 1972 by Project Test Pattern
Library of Congress Catalog Card Number: 72-80715
ISBN: 0-8164-2077-7
Text and Cover Design by Carol Basen
Printed in the United States of America

Third Printing

To
Parson Poynor, Louis Haskell, Joe Horn,
Bill Wendt, and Kyle McGee
my parish pastors;
to
The People of the Church of the Holy Family
who shared their ministry with me
1957–1969;
and
to
Everyone who cares about parishes . . .

FOREWORD ════════════════════════

Loren Mead, a pioneer experimenter and educator, is here reporting on the results of a study known as "Project Test Pattern," an experimental program designed to explore the potentialities existing in congregations. His faith in what he is doing in and through congregations is refreshing and reassuring.

Men have always congregated and always will. Our world will change; the form of the Church will probably change; but because of our nature—especially our dependence upon relationships—we will continue to seek each other out in order to be together. Congregating is our response to a need in ourselves and others and to the presence of something beyond us—the ultimate that speaks to us in all relationships. We Christians call this ultimate the Holy Spirit who reveals Jesus the Christ and his Father.

Congregating, however, is not simple. Because it is a human activity, it is fraught with complications that are peculiarly human. As Loren Mead has described, and as we all know, congregations can easily become formal, repressive,

5

sterile, and enemies of everything they profess. They may also become liabilities in local communities because they are prone to compete with each other and with other community resources rather than act in complementary ways.

New Hope for Congregations is a positive book. Instead of dwelling on what is wrong with the Church and congregations, it describes and interprets the attempts made by Project Test Pattern to understand and work with the dynamics of congregational life. A part of the wisdom of Project Test Pattern is demonstrated in the use of regional resource persons to serve as "adviser/consultants" to congregations in their general localities. How these people function is a significant contribution of this book. This corps of trained personnel work with congregations and their pastors in a variety of programs. These programs involve congregations in processes of self-examination, of decision-making, and of opening up and dealing with old and new conflicts. The gaps between clergy and laity are narrowed by the practice of two-way communication, so that congregations and clergy may help each other discover and use their respective resources. The purpose of all this effort is to free congregations and their clergy to be both *nurturing* and *witnessing* communities.

There is such desperate need for *nurturing,* sustaining groups. People are confused by changes that are coming so fast that their values and ways of life are constantly being uprooted. They are lonely, fearful, and therefore mistrustful. What a difference it would make if congregations were loving, supportive, forgiving, and compassionate! They would then indeed be embodiments of the Spirit of Christ, warm spots in the life of each community not only for their own membership but for others as well.

And the need for *witnessing* communities is desperate,

too. So much needs to be done in so many problem-filled areas of life, areas where congregations have opportunity to work together and to infiltrate society with courageous and rigorous faith and love. While many write off the Church as obsolete, it is also true that thousands of leaders in society—in business and industry, education, government, and medicine—are members of congregations who bring their questions and insights to their worship and study, and who return to their places in that society with new perspective and purpose. No one can measure the effect of the spreading, rippling response of people as they move day by day through the challenges of their areas of responsibility. This "Church in the world" is already powerful. But how much more powerful it would be if theoretical belief and daily action could reinforce one another and become one!

There exists a growing need for programs providing on-the-scene training in the participants' home situations. The at-home milieu is a source of learning, the curriculum for our most effective learnings. It is an exciting achievement when people learn to use their resources to work at their problems. Out of such experiences is born a sense of self-worth, confidence, and growth.

I invite you to read this story about hopeful congregations. It grows out of an advanced and courageous approach to an exciting new educational development that has demonstrated success in producing change and growth.

REUEL L. HOWE

PREFACE

Many people have shared the dream. Robert Brown and John Hines made it possible to begin working toward making the dream a reality.

The dream was that the local congregation, the parish church, was called to be more than it was; that the local church *could be* more than it was!

The dream, of course, is much larger than the particular shape they gave it, but their dream and how they brought it to life was important. Robert Brown, then the Episcopal Bishop of Arkansas, and John Hines, Presiding Bishop of the Episcopal Church, conceived the possibility of careful, responsible experimentation leading toward the renewal of local congregations. Through their leadership and their dreams, Project Test Pattern (PTP) was born in June 1969 as a temporary force within the Church to produce the kind of study that could be immediately put into action.

Bishops Brown and Hines did not dream in a vacuum; a great company of pioneers had preceded them, particularly after World War II—men and women motivated by a vast discomfort with the gap they saw between what the gospel was and what the local congregation was doing. Among these pioneers were men like Abbé Michonneau of Paris, George MacLeod of Iona and Glasgow, Ernest Southcott of Leeds, George Webber of Harlem, Gordon Cosby of Washington. The weaknesses of the ministry of the congregation were exposed by critics like Gibson Winter and Peter Berger. They made clear some of the basic weaknesses of the local congregation:

. . . how it had become a self-concerned, self-perpetuating organization;
. . . how it ministered comfortably to the comfortable;
. . . how its prophetic voice had become anemic;
. . . how it failed to minister to the ghetto or to the world of professional life;
. . . how it paid more and more attention to neighborhood in a world that no longer operated through neighborhoods.

Bishops Brown and Hines particularly saw their dream as related to the study of "The Missionary Structure of the Congregation" sponsored by the World Council of Churches in the early 1960s. They intended to build upon that work.

Their dream came into being at a time that was a crisis point for the churches. The rapid growth of the Church in the '50s and early '60s had begun to falter, for no reason that people could clearly identify. An enthusiasm for Christian education shifted to concern for a ministry of social action. Then that excitement ran into various kinds of backlashes—perhaps the most challenging being the realization that social ills were easier to preach about or demonstrate about than to cure. Overshadowing those concerns within the churches was the profound disillusionment that colored American life as, for the first time, the American people began to run into problems that seemed to have no solution: Vietnam, racism, poverty, environmental abuse, crime, economic "stagflation," drugs.

Caught in all these pressures, parishes had come upon hard times. Studies of parish ministers described their low morale and sense of ineffectiveness. There was considerable outflow of ordained men from parish work to teaching, social work, and related professions. Men preparing in theological seminaries indicated little desire to go into parish ministry.

In the midst of this ferment evolved Project Test Pattern, an agency committed to learning how parishes actually operate and how they could operate more effectively. Basic to that commitment was the deep conviction that something *could* be done. With that commitment and that conviction, PTP was able to try things, even things that turned out not to work very well, provided it learned from mistakes and constantly moved toward better methods.

PTP found that training for parish leaders in off-site conferences had very limited effect. At the same time it discovered that third-party assistance *in* the parish from persons skilled in such roles did have considerable impact. Refining that knowledge and continuing a process of fine-tuning it, PTP set up experimental consultative relationships between pairs of parish development adviser/consultants and "client parishes" who had chosen to work with them on their own life and work. Not all such relationships worked. In some cases the consultants and the parish simply did not hit it off. In some cases the congregation could not respond to the help offered. In some cases PTP did not provide adequate training and supervision for the consultant team. Wherever things did not go well in the change process, PTP worked to find the cause of the malfunction and to develop strategies for overcoming it.

In a number of cases, however, the client parishes found the experience useful. They achieved greater effectiveness in defining and working toward their goals as a congregation.

Where the consultation worked and where it did not, the consultants' reports of their work provided PTP with valuable insights into the dynamics of parishes—how clergy and laity interact, the difficulties church committees have in making decisions and taking action, how changes affect people in parishes, which consultant methods work and which do not. The body of information was of a kind that simply had not existed before.

Because of the value of this information to people in parishes, to clergy, to bishops and other regional church executives and their staffs, to teachers, to researchers, PTP began to find itself pressed to publish findings, often before the findings were complete. A variety of papers have been published.

This book is an attempt to make available to a broader audience the findings of the PTP network—a network that now contains some thirty project advisers and seventy parish development consultants operating from the Pacific Northwest to the Gulf Coast and to New England. I am grateful to the vestry of Trinity Parish, New York. The generosity of that vestry made it possible for PTP to share the learnings in this book.

A word of caution is in order: there is much, much more to be learned.

I need to say some personal things, too. I share the vision of Robert Brown and John Hines. I am deeply and emotionally committed to the value of the parish church. This is partly because parish churches have been such an important part of my life and partly because all the things I value most highly, the things I believe most deeply, are focused in what the local congregation is and is called to be. I am also aware of the pressure within me of my strong ties of comradeship and admiration for men I've worked with in the ordained ministry, men who have carried heavy burdens and who have been faithful in both large things and small, often with little encouragement.

On another level altogether, I also happen to believe that the local religious congregation is by far the most important social institution in the world with the possible single exception of the family. How religious congregations evolve will make an enormous difference to the kind of world that tomorrow brings.

Bishop Brown and Bishop Hines seemed to sense my commitment and have been most gracious in their support, even when my own style and passion gave their dream a different shape from that which they expected. They have been unfailing in support, but willing to press me with sharp criticism where they felt it was needed. That kind of honesty is hard to find.

Fortunately for Project Test Pattern, I soon found some people with expertise to balance my passion. Jim Anderson and Jack Harris from Washington. Carman Hunter and Al Rollins from New York. George Reynolds from Cincinnati. Bill Yon from Birmingham. Ray Averett from Baltimore.

Herb Donovan from Montclair. Jack Wyatt from Spokane.
Ken Allen from Los Angeles. Robbie Macfarlane of New
York and Los Angeles. (Robbie is the one whose word at a
crucial time led me to see the need to put this book together.) This group came into the game as technical advisers, but soon became much more than my teachers—they
became my personal support system and eventually my
management group. In that developmental process my own
consultant, Rolf Lynton of Chapel Hill, North Carolina, was
invaluable.

Elisa DesPortes came on board as my assistant for research in the summer of 1970 when I could promise her
only four months' pay. She has stayed with it through thick
and thin. (The thinnest it's been was March 31, 1971, when
we had funds for only six more days!) Elisa did all the hard
legwork to gather the data on St. Mark's and St. Michael's.
She prepared the chapters on them and on St. Bartholomew's for this book.

Celia Hahn as our editorial consultant has contributed
much to the shape of this book. Her critical eye helped us
on every page of the manuscript, but her major contribution
was her skill in identifying the message Project Test Pattern
has to tell and pressing me to be clear in telling it. Katey
Harris and Wilma Swanson of the office staff have put in
long hours of typing and retyping this book to get it out on
time. Betty Praktish, who continues to do part-time work
with us while carrying a full load at Virginia Theological
Seminary, had an important part in shaping PTP in its form-
ative period.

When all is said and done, though, I am responsible for
what is in this book. The mistakes in it are mistakes I either
made or condoned! There is one thing I genuinely hope,

however: *that whoever reads this book will find increased commitment to making his own congregation a vital unit of ministry.*

L.B.M.

Mount St. Alban
Ash Wednesday, 1972

CONTENTS

1

THE PARISH CHURCH TODAY

"Why don't you practice what you preach!" my friend challenged me. "You people in the churches—you talk big about life and love and freedom and all that, but I don't see you doing much in this town. Hell, you're just a bunch of bickering hypocrites as far as I can tell."

My carefully thought-out arguments and glib answers stuck in my throat. He and I worked together on a local community board, and I had asked him to come to my congregation to hear me preach one Sunday when I knew I had an unusually eloquent one up my sleeve. I had forgotten that we had a parish meeting scheduled immediately after the service, so he had sat through an hour-and-a-half donnybrook about whether we were going to have a flat roof or a steep-pitched roof on our new parish house. He had seen people who call themselves the Body of Christ bicker, politely insulting each other's intelligence and casting aspersions on each other's integrity. He had seen me smile grimly and pretend to be genial and all-loving, when he knew I had wanted to smash two people's heads together.

"You weren't honest for a minute in there," he went on.
"You don't act that way on our board. If you did, I wouldn't
give you the time of day. Why in the world do you all act
that way in the church? Thanks for the invitation, but it'll
be a while before I come back!"

He had me dead to rights. Neither the congregation nor I
had been living the way we professed to. I had been in that
spot before, and I have been in it a lot since. I never found
it a very comfortable spot to be in.

THE GAP BETWEEN PERFORMANCE
AND POTENTIAL

Sunday in, Sunday out, millions of Americans get up, put
on their Sunday best, and head off for an hour or two at
their local parish church.[1] On a given day there will be
thousands of folk songs sung and guitars plucked, organs
pumped or played, anthems offered, chants chanted, masses
said, prayers prayed, sermons preached, offerings received,
as corporate actions by those millions. These things will
happen in magnificent museumlike buildings in the concrete
caverns of our great cities; they will happen in storefront
missions a few blocks away; they will happen in tum-
bledown, termite-ridden wooden churches where rural poverty is a way of life; they will happen in centuries-old adobe

[1] In this book the words "parish," "local church," and "congregation"
are used interchangeably. This is to avoid too narrow a definition, since
most of us use the words rather loosely. We might be aware, however,
that there are connotations of each that are mutually enriching—*parish*,
connoting an area of turf under the care of the ministry; *local church*, the
concrete location and place, including buildings and grounds; *congregation*, the people associated with that particular community of faith. Let
the meanings interpenetrate, even though "congregation" will be the pre-
vailing connotation.

churches and in glass and plastic structures that look like banks; they will sometimes happen in school buildings or private homes with moveable furniture. The words said will be in Spanish, English, French, Polish, Ukrainian dialects, Norwegian, German, and as many other tongues as people speak. The Christians who go to those local parish churches are white and black and brown and yellow and red.

The churchgoing habit is not as popular as it was a few years ago, yet it remains a major phenomenon pondered by sociologists, anthropologists, city planners, politicians, theologians, and also by those who dislike or disbelieve what those parish churches stand for.

Almost all the people who get up on Sunday mornings to go to their church and almost all the people who try to figure out why they do it know about the uncomfortable gap my friend reproached me with—the gap between what the local congregation preaches and what it practices.

The local parish church as experienced by most Christians, lay and ordained alike, leaves very much to be desired. The evidence of their week-by-week experience is that many local congregations are unclear about their tasks and ineffective in accomplishing them. The individual Christian finds himself or herself in an uncomfortable bind, with his or her basic beliefs contradicted by the way the congregation *acts*.

Caricatures abound that point to the obvious weaknesses in the way many congregations do act:

The Edifice Complex. A fixation on newer, bigger, more elaborate physical plants. (Larger and larger barns to contain less and less grain!)

Recreation-itis. The tendency to spend more and more time and energy providing recreational outlets—scouting, dancing, bridge, etc.—for people who already have access to plenty.

The Theological Vacuum. The ability to speak profoundly about everything except the things of God and the ways of God—a kind of embarrassment about the transcendent dimension of life.

Moral Fundamentalism. The substitution of a set of moral rules for the freedom of the gospel—rules often derived from culturally rooted customs rather than from scriptural imperatives.

The Keep-Things-Cool Concept. The conviction that no one should disagree openly with anyone else. (It's better to seethe inwardly, withdraw pledges, or leave in a huff.)

The Intellectualist Fallacy. The belief that one can change a situation by voicing a new idea, even in a sermon.

The Traditionalist Idolatry. Justification of one's beliefs by statements like: "If it was good enough for my grandfather. . . ."

The Relevance Kick. The idea that anything is valid if it is up-to-date.

The Bigger Budget Fixation. The operating principle that a congregation exists to support an ever-increasing budget.

Obviously these are caricatures. Few congregations exhibit all of these characteristics, but most of us recognize enough truth in one or two to be fairly uncomfortable. Anyone who has recently sat through a long parish committee meeting is likely to remember an illustration of at least one of these caricatures, and even, perhaps, be able to add to the list!

The strange thing is that the people *in* congregations rarely *like* to exhibit such behavior. They feel trapped, unable to free their congregation from its hang-ups. These caricatures are repugnant to what they believe, but they do not know how to get free of the traps.

How very many of these binds exist in the life of the congregation! Irrelevant things seem to claim so much attention. How little energy is left to think about tasks of nurture or witness! How much energy is needed just to keep the organization's wheels barely turning! The organizational life so often seems to deplete people, absorb them, wear them out. The clergy seem harried, frustrated, often spending more and more time doing things they think of as peripheral to their calling. How little energy is left over for facing out in witness!

Of course this is not the whole story. Every congregation has some people whose lives reflect their commitment to Jesus, and no congregation is completely bereft of the works of ministry. But often those concerns have a hard time getting onto the agenda of the parish board at its monthly meeting.

In its corporate life, the parish often becomes an institution of frightened people. It becomes defensive, self-protective—the very antithesis of the loving freedom proclaimed by the gospel and believed by many of its members. It is this bind that is so discouraging to the Christian—to be committed to Jesus Christ, yet trapped in a corporate body that negates that gospel. The very fellowship that exists to support them in their faith is bound up in ways of living that deny the fellowship's goals.

How demoralizing it can be to be part of such a congregation—having such concern for its life, caring so much for the gospel of Jesus Christ and finding the corporate life further and further away from that gospel. No wonder clergy

drop out in profound disillusionment. No wonder enthusiastic lay persons sometimes drift into passivity or drop away
quietly.

The peculiar thing that strikes observers is that almost
every parish seems to have a wealth of unused resources
within it. Every congregation has numbers of people whose
lives have been deeply touched by the gospel and who are
quite serious in their desire to respond in faithful action.
There are those who sit in pews out of habit; there are others who do so to go along with social custom or to preserve
family peace; but there are also a vast number who see their
local congregation as a community that is in touch with the
most important meanings in their lives. Such people contribute sacrificially of their time and energy and also of their
money. Such people will sit through hour after hour of dull
committee meetings hoping against hope that new life will
come to their parish. The importance of Jesus Christ to
them makes them put up with frustration and weariness
that would confound the saints!

The man in the pulpit often reflects the same qualities.
He bears scars—scars of frustration and of disappointed
hopes. He has mixed motives for being where he is, and the
chances are that he is bone-weary with the whole thing. He
often holds on only because he, too, has been touched by
the power of God. He, too, seeks to work out a faithful response to what God has done in his life.

John Milton, speaking in another age, said of the people
in the pew looking up to the pulpit: "The hungry sheep look
up and are not fed." In our time the hungry sheep and the
hungry shepherd are one. In their hunger they seek ways to
break their congregations out of unfreedom to become
nourishing communities of faith.

THE EMERGENCE OF PARISH DEVELOPMENT

The gap between the actual performance of the local congregation and its potential has been a growing concern for those who live in congregations and also for those who have the care of the churches—the bishops and other officials who have responsibility for providing support services for congregations and clergy in a region.

The parish has a hard time breaking out of its trap. A variety of techniques and methods have been attempted—new forms of meetings for revival or witnessing, structural changes, mergers of congregations, several strategies of leadership training. None has had much success in making congregations more effective in doing their tasks, although some of the methods have brought gospel-freedom to some individuals.

Since 1969 Project Test Pattern has been carrying out in-depth experimentation and research in local congregations to find ways to free them for their work of ministry. The research has had the double goal of learning about the complex inner life of congregations and of *actualizing* more effective units of ministry. PTP has developed a network of some seventy parish development adviser/consultants who work in pairs with congregations all over the United States. These teams work under contract with individual local congregations to bring greater clarity and effectiveness to the work of those congregations. At the same time the teams are producing records of the dynamics of the congregation's inner life and interactions. A body of careful observations about what actually happens in parishes is gradually build-

ing up—observations that help identify the binds and traps
and that help discover effective ways of achieving breakthroughs to freedom at those points.

Project Test Pattern is only one part of a larger and almost amorphous movement growing simultaneously in a
number of denominations and areas in America. Several regional and national church bodies have become concerned
for what is called "parish development," and a number of
training programs have been designed to train "parish development consultants." In several areas regional staff people have become Directors of Parish Development.

Several presuppositions seem to be held in common by
those concerned for parish development:

1. There is a belief that congregational life can be more
effective and satisfying than it generally is.

2. Each parish is seen to be a unique system of relationships.

3. The process of changing congregations is seen as involving much time and energy.

4. Parish adviser/consultants are used in the change process of each parish.

Project Test Pattern's research in parish development is
uncovering information about parish life that has not been
available before. This book is an attempt to share some of
that information, together with our first hypotheses about
what we can learn from it. This is done in the conviction
that the truth is indeed a force of freedom.

Parish development can only be told in stories. What happens as one congregation moves through its own history is
literally unrepeatable. How one congregation moves toward
fulfilling its own ministry is related to the particular people
who are involved, the opportunities or challenges to minis-

try, the particular traps that have developed in the congregation's own history.

For these reasons it is important to read stories of parish development, not to learn *what* happens, but to learn *how* it happens. It is important to see *how* one event relates to others, *how* decisions get made—not *what* the event or the decisions were. It is the process of development itself that is transferable to other congregations, not the actual events. And it is the process that can be adapted or improved for use in the development of other parishes. If we can learn to use these processes, each parish can learn how to affirm the uniqueness of its own ministry.

We have stories to tell.[2] They are stories about four congregations that tried to face their own bondage and move beyond. These are not particularly unusual parishes, but some unusual things have come to happen in them. They are not now where they were when they started their journey of development, and there is evidence that they are all stronger bases of ministry than when they started. Project Test Pattern initiated the process in two of the cases, it became involved in the continuation of the process in another, and it did the research to find the story in all four cases.

[2] These stories are narratives drawn from the research files PTP has gathered to study the technical processes of change in congregations. Several other articles, papers, research documents, and consultant resources have been published from those files. (For further information write: Project Test Pattern, Mount Saint Alban, Washington, D.C. 20016.)

2

THE STORY OF ST. MICHAEL'S

A NEW MINISTER IN A DISCOURAGED CONGREGATION

St. Michael and All Angels' Church, Adelphi, Maryland, founded in the boom of optimism of the 1950s, was a small Episcopal congregation that never seemed to fulfill the promise of its earliest years. Located in a highly mobile suburban community a few miles northwest of Washington, D.C., St. Michael's borders on a massive beltway that surrounds the city and connects the suburbs. Although the Diocesan[1] Missions Committee had advised against founding this mission, St. Michael's grew rapidly in its early years due to the leadership of effective clergymen and lay leaders. After seventeen years of life, however, membership, money, and morale were low.

In 1965 the Rev. Ronald Albaugh became St. Michael's third rector. As one parishioner describes that period: "When Ron came we were at the bottom—at our lowest point. It was very possible that we would go bankrupt. There was much dissension and divisiveness. A lot of people

[1] The diocese is the regional unit of the Episcopal Church, led by a bishop and his staff.

were losing interest, hoping the problems would go away, or just hanging on and gritting their teeth. When Ron opened the lid, he got a can of worms. But he saw the possibilities that were buried underneath."

Trying to bring new life, Albaugh initiated an annual vestry[2] conference, a new education program, and a youth group. He began experimenting with Sunday morning worship held "in the round." The experience proved to be disastrous—the congregation was split for and against the worship experiment, and St. Michael's seemed paralyzed by the polarization that resulted. Charged with emotional build-up and tension, the whole issue of worship remained an unresolved conflict. It seemed that every attempt to bring new life to St. Michael's simply brought new troubles. Albaugh communicated his discouragement and bafflement through his style of leadership. One parishioner remembers him as floundering and feeling that St. Michael's was moving toward death.

DEFINING AND WORKING ON THE PROBLEM

In the fall of 1968, Albaugh asked the Rev. James D. Anderson from the Washington Diocesan Office of Parish Development to lead a vestry conference to clarify his role and job as rector. Rather than lead a conference, Mr. Anderson agreed to meet with the rector and a vestry committee to find out the problems and to decide what would be the most appropriate way to resolve them.

Meeting several times, the group decided the principal problem was Albaugh's own confusion about himself and his

[2] The vestry is the governing body of a local Episcopal congregation.

ministry. On Anderson's recommendation he attended the
Northeast Career Center at Princeton, N.J., in February
1969. Albaugh came through this rigorous but supportive
experience feeling affirmed in his skills, committed to the
parish ministry and St. Michael's, and more open to the possibility of receiving additional help to work on problems
that were interfering with his effectiveness. He continued to
work on personal renewal as a necessary adjunct to parish
renewal.

After tackling the initial problem of Ron Albaugh's confusion, the vestry and rector felt ready for the weekend conference. One vestryman described their problems: "Vestry
meetings were terrible. We weren't getting any work done.
Ron distrusted his abilities. We were to write a job description, but we couldn't even adopt an agenda. We were par-
rots, repeating what had just been said. Where were we to
go?" Mr. Anderson, serving as consultant, described the first
session of the vestry weekend as "history night." The atmosphere was pervaded with sentimentality and nostalgia.
Older members were yearning for a lost past, while newer
ones were resentful and detached. In the midst of this very
submerged conflict, the rector was still trying to discover his
own role as leader.

On Saturday the rector began to lead a discussion on
parish concerns. After a good deal of struggle, the group
bogged down. They never returned to the agenda; rather,
they looked at what was going on among themselves. For
the first time the group began to be able to speak more directly and honestly. One participant described the consultant's help: "Jim would say, 'Stop! No one is listening!' and
he would point to examples. From that we turned to, 'How
do we feel about each other?' We were crucifying each

other. We saw what we were doing to each other, and we began to move to a personal level."

On Sunday the vestry were able to list some issues that concerned them: "What do we do about conflict?" "How do we reach decisions?" "How do we communicate effectively within the parish?" "How do we keep from forgetting what we have learned this weekend?" The weekend ended in a climate of optimism and hope because the participants found they could face their problems without folding up. One vestryman described the help Anderson provided: "For once there was some expertise on the job. It was the first time we had had a detached individual who had professional knowledge of how people operate. The big thing was getting out on the table feelings that were otherwise concealed. This renewal would not have gotten sparked without this outside help. Jim Anderson's professional touch helped us get a sense of how to go about getting this parish together."

Mr. Anderson did not lead the weekend, but served as consultant. He compares the consultant's job to that of a coach—the coach does not play the game, he helps the players practice fundamentals and use their skills in scrimmage. He helps the players learn from their experience by looking at how they played in the past.

SOME TANGIBLE RESULTS

With Mr. Anderson continuing to meet with the rector and the vestry to work on their problems, the group initiated a vestry notebook and more structured agenda for meetings in order to provide more orderliness. The rector became more vigorous in his leadership by solidly endorsing

the diocesan fund-raising campaign for missionary development. The vestry committee involved itself totally with
much hard work and detailed planning. St. Michael's raised
$18,000, 106 per cent of its quota. After repeated experi-
ences of failure in achieving objectives, this success was a
significant boost to parish morale.

During the same spring of 1969, the vestry, realizing how
little they knew of the actual feeling and opinions of parishioners, developed a two-night parish planning meeting to
bridge that gap. With Anderson's assistance, parishioners
shared what made life exciting for them and what pro-
hibited life from being rewarding.

The vestry took all the suggestions, built a new set of
priorities, and planned a course of action. Worship and
youth headed the list. The vestry chose to begin with youth,
a less controversial issue than worship. They hired Mrs. Jean
Haldane, the Diocesan Consultant on Youth, to work with
the rector and a committee composed of equal numbers of
young people and adults.

WORKING TOGETHER PAYS OFF

The Youth and Adult Committee began by planning one
event to see if young people and adults had anything to say
to each other. As one forty-year-old explained: "As an adult,
I personally felt separated from young people. I didn't know
any of them, nor did I know how to talk to them."

Discovering that the young people and adults were surprised at how much they enjoyed being together and how
much they needed each other, the Youth and Adult Committee spent its first year planning events that enabled
young people and adults to grow together. The members
worked developmentally, taking one step at a time. They

would decide on a clear objective (such as youth and adult communication), plan and design an event, and then evaluate the experience to see where to move next. One sixteen-year-old committee member described Jean Haldane's help: "We would get in ruts just sitting around and not saying anything. Jean enabled us to do work that we wanted to do but didn't know how. She helped us understand what was happening and helped us move."

In the spring of 1970, the parish voted by a five-to-one majority to incorporate young people into the decision-making bodies of the parish by giving voting rights and election privileges to sixteen-year-olds. A seventeen-year-old girl, a member of the Youth and Adult Planning Committee, was elected to the vestry.

No longer was there an atmosphere of "adults doing something for the kids" or of kids "being put down." One sixteen-year-old boy describes the change this way: "I was not involved before the Youth and Adult Committee. I hated coming to church, and the Sunday night program was boring. Now when I speak I know I will be treated as a person, not just a kid, and will be taken seriously because I have responsibility. We don't feel overpowered by adults now. It just sort of happened. Even on the outside I am a lot more open now. I never used to tell anybody anything. Now I talk about things."

The Youth and Adult Committee, wanting to involve the entire parish in what committee members were experiencing, planned and held a worship service to conclude their first year together in June 1970. It was much more than just another "Youth Service" tolerated by adults. The senior warden, expressing the feelings of most of St. Michael's, said, "I have never participated in a more satisfying and moving worship service as an adult!"

The work of the Youth and Adult Committee had a strong impact on the whole parish. One adult in the committee observed the reactions of parishioners. He explained: "Our life created an awareness in people. It showed parishioners that here is a group that really has their stuff together. They really can do something. People observed that young people and adults were talking to each other."

Homegrown programs, though more real than "canned ones," require a great deal of effort, attention, and hard work. The whole experience was remembered by one young member as, "Blood, sweat, and tears; the joy, beauty, and great accomplishment that came from working on the Youth and Adult Committee; the moments when, in conversation with different persons, I felt we met each other as persons."

WORKING ON WORSHIP: PARISH IDENTITY

In the late fall of 1969, as the Youth and Adult Committee began work with Jean Haldane, the vestry and rector spent another weekend together with Mr. Anderson serving as consultant. He brought with him the Rev. H. Barry Evans, a parish clergyman interested in liturgical consultation, who had been hired by the vestry in the late summer to consult with a task force on worship.

Working with Barry Evans and Jim Anderson, the vestry and rector were seized with a new idea: that their old problem of worship was integrally related to their corporate identity. Sunday morning worship was seen as an effort to find and express their identity. It should appropriately reflect their life together. Growing optimistic, they firmly committed themselves to that new vision and applied for a grant from the diocesan fund to help pay the consultant's fees. As Barry Evans summarized it: "We saw a need to spend an extended period of time, perhaps a year, on the hard work of congregational problem-solving, focusing on worship as the center of parish life, the goal being to develop a clear identity for St. Michael's as a parish." Mr. Anderson described his feelings about the vestry's work: "Things began to jell. It felt like it was going to work."

The Worship Task Force, with Mr. Evans consulting, committed itself to developing an effective process for liturgical renewal, rather than merely planning worship services. Working with the congregation on Sunday mornings, the Worship Task Force came to a consensus that its effort should be to "enrich the familiar" rather than adopt what was currently fashionable in other churches. The members of the congregation directed Mr. Albaugh to use silent meditations at specific points in the worship service in order to help them reflect on the words they had heard so often.

From this point on, the group worked diligently to discover their individual and corporate needs for worship. Coming up with individual needs was not an easy task. One member described their initial attempt: "I often said, 'Barry, I wish you would lead.' Barry would respond, 'I wish you would lead.' It took me awhile to see it. He has a socratic way of doing things. It enabled me to give birth to my own ideas. Now I'm convinced that is the only way it can be done. Others' ideas are not my own. They just don't fit."

LOOKING AT THEIR TOTAL LIFE

The 1969–1970 year was a good one at St. Michael's. As one young member put it: "Over the past nine months the parish community seems to have been able to start trying things when we are not sure what the outcome will be, to have gotten the courage and faith in people to do what we know we have to do. During the same time I have been feeling gradually more free here, personally, like this is the one place I can often let go."

As St. Michael's matured with so much happening in different areas of parish life, the rector and the consultants met regularly to assess the over-all pattern. They would look at the issues, try to spot where resistances occurred, and figure out the meaning of specific incidents. They worked at keeping the roles of the consultants clear, making sure that the responsibility for decisions and actions was in the hands of the parish. Jim Anderson firmly believes in the importance of regularly examining what is happening to the parish as a whole. "Paying attention to the total system was crucial. When we did not do it, things came unglued, and we paid the consequences."

The vestry met again in the summer of 1970 to review their life together and evaluate what was happening. With Anderson consulting, the group again got a fix on where they were and where they wanted to go. The use of consultants was becoming a way of life for St. Michael's. The senior warden, skeptical at first, described his appreciation for an outside consultant: "Things began to change about the time we got consultants. Jim may not have answers, but he has damn good questions. Like, 'What the hell is going on?' We would get so involved and wrapped up in our prejudices and biases. He has a way of moving you from discussions to decisions. He is also good at getting stalled discussions going, summarizing and getting us to move."

Another vestryman sees consultation as only natural: "I don't know why churches don't like to be like life. I've used consultants for thirty-one years in business." He went on to speak about the changes in his own life because St. Michael's was coming alive: "What's been going on here has built my hopes that I can learn to live as a Christian in the outside world. My boss goes to church and comes back acting like a maniac. Here there is a real caring about people that carries over. I put more joy in giving now. I want to give money to St. Michael's instead of to the race track."

A different opinion is held by still another vestryman: "I was hostile to the consultants at first and came away with a low opinion. I later felt that at least they were helping us keep on track. Gradually I saw that they could do some other things, like prompting us to express ideas, but I still feel that, except for a big problem, we can take care of it by ourselves."

MOVING OUT

For the 1970–1971 season the Youth and Adult Committee, the rector, and Mrs. Haldane committed themselves to working together for another year. The committee wanted to get involved in the community and spent months researching the geographical area around St. Michael's, trying to decide what "community" really meant to them and what they had to offer. After a great deal of effort, they found they were stuck. As Jean Haldane commented: "The group faced a difficult decision. They had put a lot of time, effort, and energy into their work. A decision to shift directions was a very maturing and a great learning experience for them. They grew to know what they could and could not do." The Youth and Adult Committee redefined "community" as friends, relatives, and neighbors, and its members concentrated on sharing some of their learnings and growth with people they knew.

As September approached, Mrs. Haldane told the com-

mittee members that, because of other commitments, the
time she had to spend at St. Michael's would be limited.
Some members became very angry and upset by her news.
Finally they came to realize that they really could handle
their life by themselves, and that it would benefit both parties if Mrs. Haldane were less involved in the parish. She
would continue to consult with the Youth and Adult Committee occasionally, when needed. The group made two
plans for their future: (1) To design something for the whole
congregation to take part in. (Exclusiveness had been a necessary condition at the start, but now they wanted to widen
their horizons.) (2) To join with other churches who had
youth and adult projects in order to become a center where
youth and adult work could be fostered and explored.

During 1970–1971, St. Michael's also worked diligently
on the worship issue. Building on the work of the previous
year, with Barry Evans consulting, the Worship Task Force
members concentrated on their individual and corporate
needs. One incident occurred during an overnight conference that came to be called the group's own legend. For a
time the task force bogged down in generalizations. Finally
one woman broke through with her personal feelings. She
told the group that when she first arrived at church, she
wanted to be alone. She needed to spend time in quietness
and prayer, participating in the liturgy quite personally,
until later in the service when she felt free to relate to other
people. Being the mother of four teenagers, her own life was
extremely active and energetic, filled with heavy responsibilities and pressures. She often stayed up late after the family retired to get time for peace and quiet. After they had
heard her story, the group could respect and value her
needs, even if they did not feel the same needs.

After the group had explored her concern for a while, the

rector, needing to present the other side of the picture, said that when he came to worship he needed to get in touch with people before he could worship in comfort, to see them, speak to them, touch them, and renew his sense of the community and his place in it. Members of the group responded to these offerings by discovering that their differences did not divide them. In a report to the vestry they shared their learnings: "What the task force has come to believe is that it is important to take seriously any need expressed in any way. At the same time, it is important to find out more about the need in order to understand it better. Invariably the 'presenting need' has something of great depth and importance to the individual behind it. What is being searched for here is a person's motivation for worshiping, one's personal stake."

After Christmas the rector provided confident, clear leadership for a new liturgical experience. Initially uneasy about how the congregation would take a discussion during sermon time, he prepared a three-page explanation. Seconds before the sermon hymn, he threw it away, telling himself, "I am going to lead them instead of coaxing and defending. I have got to ask them to risk following my leadership, instead of convincing them of the steps before we can go. All of a sudden, I realized that I was looking at the people as the enemy. Fortunately I was able to come to terms with the leadership pressures I was feeling and communicate to the members of the congregation that I trusted them to take the risk."

JOURNEYING ON AT A "HUMAN PACE"

By the first weekend in April 1971, the time was ripe for St. Michael's to reap the harvest of all its hard work and experience. More than seventy members of the parish came together for a weekend conference, led by the Worship Task Force, to explore the possibility of making a "liturgical journey" together. Said the rector, "I feel we are prepared by the kind of life we now have to move into a whole new period—a liturgical period—to pull together all of our growth and worship in a new kind of level of life. It is important to me that we do this work together, that we work at a human pace, and that no one gets left behind."

The participants, many of them young people, broke up into small discussion groups and brought back questions they had. They plastered the walls with newsprint. There were many reservations and questions about the liturgical exploration. As Barry Evans pointed out: "The small-group work had succeeded in revealing some substantial differences within the congregation. Some attempt was made to reconcile the points of view that evening, but it only seemed to make things worse. Some people were already moving, anxious to begin making some changes. Others had reservations about the whole idea of a liturgical journey. And no group was really ready to listen to another. The meeting ended in frustration."

After the meeting, Evans, Albaugh, and the task force got together to try to answer the question: "What am I really letting myself in for when I say 'Yes' to the journey?" They came up with the following answers: (1) expressing my ideas and feelings, even when they are unpopular; (2) listening to others, even when I don't want to be open to new ideas; (3) being open to the general idea of change, without committing myself in advance to any particular change; (4) facing differences with honesty, rather than pushing them aside and smoothing them over; (5) learning how to make decisions by consensus; (6) facing, exploring, and answering the question, "Why?"

A layman compared the liturgical journey to a prospecting trip: "We think there is gold out there. Perhaps we will find it. We now understand it in terms of discovery instead of change." This explanation of the idea of the journey, by its simple clarity, acted as a catalyst to draw the community together. The group decided that they had reached a consensus and were ready to move forward.

The rest of their time together was spent brainstorming ideas for making the liturgy more satisfying. One plan that everybody was enthusiastic about was to replace the hard-backed pews with movable and comfortable chairs. Several committees were formed to investigate the possibilities of new chairs and other specific areas of improvement. They wound up the conference on Palm Sunday with a celebrative worship service, united in a spirit of community and adventure, but freed to express reservations and differences and committed to listening to each other. St. Michael's liturgical journey had well begun.

Soon after the parish weekend, the committees began to meet. The Seating Committee developed a way of working in relation to the congregation that avoided vote-taking and allowed parishioners to move when they were ready. Different styles of chairs were displayed on Sunday mornings for members to look at and sit in. The committee carefully assessed the reactions. Finally, one chair was found that seemed to please most people. The rector announced that fifty chairs would be purchased with parish funds, but if anyone wished to supplement that with their own funds, those contributions would be gratefully received. There was no pressure, no campaign—but the order signed in July was for eighty chairs!

The importance of the "chair decision" was not the actual order for new chairs but the way that decision was made—smoothly, personally, and with everybody on board. Jim Anderson pointed out, "In light of the history of this parish, the decisions that were made about worship, chairs, and liturgy were indeed the climax and culmination of this parish's entire liturgical project. Three and a half years ago, it would have been impossible for St. Michael's to make such a decision. The progress and growth that it has made in the past two years is absolutely remarkable."

In September 1971, St. Michael's rector, vestry, and chief consultant, Jim Anderson, met for a two-night session to go over their history, look at their over-all operations, and get clear about what was going on. Concerns about the exclusiveness and prestige of the Worship Task Force were aired. The work of the Community Concerns Project, the educational program, and the Women's Group was discussed—all of which had developed styles of operation similar to those of the Youth and Adult Committee and the Worship Task Force.[3] They felt that St. Michael's was quite different from what it had been a few years ago. One vestrywoman described her feelings about the changed atmosphere: "Personally we began to be people-oriented rather than task-oriented. I used to suppress my personal wishes for the task or goal. I used to be afraid to oppose an idea because of fear of opposing the person. Now I have learned to reject an idea and not the person. Now when we work on a task we enjoy it and are enriched by it. I learned that those little aspects of me really count. The consultants enabled me to be creative.

[3] Due to space limitations, this study presents only the processes of the vestry, the Youth and Adult Committee, and the Worship Task Force. Other important projects at St. Michael's included the education program, the Women's Group, and the Community Concerns Project.

They opened the door to help me get in touch with all the 'goodies' that I have."

Young people and adults are broadening their base to include other churches. The parish has committed itself to an effective ministry in the community, working through the structure of the Silver Spring Group Ministry. Because they have come to terms with their own personal needs and life in this congregation, St. Michael's members are now experiencing freedom to move out beyond their own parish.

St. Michael's was and is a parish on a journey. The journey began with the parish's beginning, but it was held up by roadblocks along the way. At several points the road seemed to be a dead end, and sometimes the parish lost its sense of direction. The people of St. Michael's were able to ask for help to find their way, and to look for the most satisfying ways of reaching their destination.

It is important to St. Michael's to pay attention to the quality of their life—to pay attention to what they do to each other along the way. It is not an easy task to make sure that everyone, no matter how different, is on board. It takes patience and persistence. The journey is not without struggle and tension. Sometimes the people lose their bearings. Sometimes they forget their history. Sometimes one group begins to leave the others behind. In spite of the difficulties, St. Michael's has persisted in its journey. By learning to meet their own human needs the people of St. Michael's have been freed to move out and bring others in. They have been freed to risk taking new paths. Journeying at a human pace has become a way of life at St. Michael's.

ELISA L. DES PORTES

3

THE STORY OF
ST. BARTHOLOMEW'S

A LIVELY CONGREGATION

For nearly fifty families in Florence, Alabama, St. Bartholomew's Episcopal Church is one of the most exciting places in town. Located on a spacious lot in a growing suburb, St. Bartholomew's has a modern parish building and a church with movable chairs and bright, modern banners hanging from the ceiling. During the weekdays, young children play on the swings outside while attending St. Bartholomew's kindergarten. On Sundays, parishioners gather for worship and church school in an informal, relaxed atmosphere. Many are young families who prefer a casual, freer atmosphere in comparison to that of Trinity Church, a more traditional downtown parish.

St. Bartholomew's considers its greatest quality to be the friendliness, warmth, and openness of the congregation. As one new member described it: "St. Bartholomew's is a real Christian community. They are a group of people who do love each other and who do care. If you come here, you will get involved. All people do. I had been here one month when I was asked to do a big job. I was immediately pulled into the activities. I didn't have to wait, and that was the greatest part." Another recent communicant put it this way: "I was surprised that my husband joined St. Bartholomew's. He is so conservative, but we joined because we felt so at home here. There is a real loving involvement."

Besides the young children and parents, St. Bartholomew's also has an active group of young people. Although they have a youth group on Sunday nights, the young people participate in all the parish projects and events. One high school girl commented on her reasons for attending St. Bartholomew's: "I dropped in here and stayed. It's a very friendly place. I can wear blue jeans. Dicky [the rector] wears blue jeans. Here you can wear anything you want. People aren't bearing down on you here. At other places I've been, it was a fashion parade. So many of us here are just plain casual." Another teenager expressed her enthusiasm: "I can't get enough of this church. Here at St. Bart's you have a feeling of God loving you instead of God hating you. I'm not scared of going to Hell now, not scared of the Devil here."

The rector, the Rev. John R. Gilchrist, thirty-three years old, also reflects the style of the parish. He is described by many parishioners as friendly and enthusiastic, open to change and willing to let the congregation make its own decisions. He is willing to abide by a majority vote rather than push through his ideas. One member explained: "Dick likes for the laymen to administer the cup, but the worship committee said, 'No,' so the decision was a 'No' decision. He believes in the priesthood of all believers." One new member, a high school teacher, commented: "I joined St. Bartholomew's because of Dick Gilchrist. I met him through a friend and liked him right off. He seemed so relaxed and friendly, fully alive. Being a black man, I wondered if there was a place where people were not torn up. I wanted a place where people don't just say they don't hate, but where people *do* actually love. I found that this church was really like Dick Gilchrist, and that he wasn't the only guy in town who was involved. This place is like a UN family. It's great because no one dominates the church. I can't tell who is the boss."

PTP CONSULTANTS BEGIN WORK

After hearing about PTP at a diocesan meeting and then reading a case history of renewal through consultation, Dick Gilchrist asked the Bishop of Alabama to nominate St. Bartholomew's as a possible congregation for using consultants. Although he considered St. Bartholomew's a young, alive parish in tune with the issues, Gilchrist felt that consultation could help the parishioners clarify their goals and communicate better. He shared his enthusiasm with Harry Pritchett, a PTP consultant and fellow clergyman in that diocese. By April 1970, the consultant team of the Rev. Harry Pritchett and Mrs. Martha Adams set up a meeting at St. Bartholomew's to explore the possibility of working at that parish.

Mr. Pritchett, a thirty-five-year-old clergyman, is rector of a church in Huntsville, Alabama, one hour from Florence. Mrs. Adams, also from Huntsville and approximately the same age, is a vivacious mother of five. Like Harry Pritchett, she has had a great deal of experience working in human relations. Both are accredited professional members of the Association of Religion and Applied Behavioral Sciences. Both consultants were also trained by Project Test Pattern in parish consultation, particularly in a field called "organization development."

The consultant team gathered information about St. Bartholomew's at their initial meeting with the rector and senior warden.[1] The congregation had been founded eight years earlier as a mission[2] of Trinity Church. It had about a hundred members, and the present rector had been there for one year. Later in the evening the consultants met with the Board of Trustees[3] to discuss the possibility of a consultation. The trustees shared their frustrations and hopes for St. Bartholomew's. Other churches were booming. They wondered what they were doing to "turn people off." Another general concern was that they felt they were involved in so many things that they could not function effectively in any one area. They felt a need to set priorities. The trustees were concerned about the mission's financial problems. There had been no significant increase in financial giving over the past few years.

The consultants, taking great care to explain their approach, used an analogy to counseling to show differences of consulting style. One kind of counselor administers psychological tests and then gives the results back to the patient, telling him what his problem is. Another works directly with the patient, helping him figure out his problem and then work on it. Pritchett and Adams stated that they chose the second way of working. They would not give answers, but would help St. Bartholomew's to identify its problems clearly, to develop a way to solve the problems and to achieve more of its potential.

Following these first meetings the consultants noted among some of their hunches that they "got some sort of un-

[1] The senior warden and the junior warden are the chief lay leaders of Episcopal congregations.

[2] A mission is a partially subsidized congregation.

[3] In some Episcopal dioceses the leadership group of the congregation is called a Board of Trustees.

easy feeling that the mission in some ways looks at itself as being very open, very 'with it,' and yet that stance does not quite ring true. It is almost as though 'the lady doth protest too much!' "

After serious consideration the consultants and the trustees agreed on a contract for a consultation. It involved a fee for professional services and travel. The consultants felt that the first thing they needed to do was to help the parish get a clearer understanding of itself. Each member needed to express his or her viewpoint and find out what others were thinking. The consultants decided the initial step should be a diagnosis of the parish's assets and talents, along with its problems and frustrations. They planned a two-night parish meeting on July 8 and 9, 1970.

Thirty-five per cent of the congregation gathered at the parish hall to give their ideas about what made life rewarding at St. Bartholomew's and also what prevented life from being more satisfying. Each participant was encouraged to make suggestions and was assured that his or her opinions would be taken seriously. Questions about the rector's leadership, the communications network, who goes to whom for what, and mixed and ambiguous responsibilities were all weighed. A high degree of frustration and confusion developed during the first night's work because of the great many negative opinions. Typical responses were: "Gosh, I must be naive. I thought we were moving along so happily." "We ought to have equal time for the positive things about this parish."

A year and a half later, one parishioner, reflecting on that first night, summarized her feelings: "After the first night there was utter confusion. I wondered how we could ever put the pieces back together again, but we did. Something happened. When Dick first came to St. Bartholomew's, we tried to establish goals, but we never followed through on them."

After the first night the consultants gathered all the ideas and grouped them into categories of specific interest and concern. Looking at the present parish committees (which were, in effect, nonexistent) the consultants realized that St. Bartholomew's, a small parish, did not have any organized committees that could take the concerns and plan concrete actions. They did not have a way to produce responsible, satisfying results. Harry and Martha saw that a critical decision had to be made. In spite of their agreement to help the parish help itself, the consultants decided to risk "doing something *for* the parish" by creating some working committees.

The second night was spent having people assign themselves to five interest groups that had been derived from the list of concerns and questions. People went to: (1) program committee, (2) worship, (3) evangelism, (4) Christian education, or (5) outreach. Each interest group agreed to arrive at two sets of goals, one to be realized in three months, the other to be realized in six months (January 1, 1971).

By the end of the second night, the atmosphere was somewhat more hopeful. One member put it this way: "It was great. It was the first time we ever took an organized look at ourselves. I was amazed at the list of things that people liked and did not like. More people became involved than ever before." Dick Gilchrist put it this way: "The flow of events brought out loads of information, but along with it hostility at the consultants for 'bringing up all this negativity.' The really exciting thing was that it did not stop there. The anxiety about 'exposing our negative feelings' was translated into action steps that would help resolve the concerns."

Continuing to gather more specific information, Martha
Adams and Harry Pritchett administered a brief questionnaire (which they had checked out beforehand with the rector) to the trustees at their July 28 meeting. The role of the
rector, who was out of town and absent from the meeting,
was the central focus. The trustees listed what the rector
did that they liked and what he did that they did not like.
They also listed what they wished him to do. A more detailed questionnaire on the style of leadership in the parish
was given to the senior warden to fill out. The same questionnaire was later given to the rector to fill out. The consultants also filled out the questionnaire. When the consultants, rector, and warden compared their responses, the
rector was able to raise some questions about his style of
leadership and its effect on the congregation. Gilchrist
firmly believed in the parishioners' taking responsibility for
their parish life, but he began to wonder if his actions really
reflected his belief.

IDENTIFYING AND WORKING
ON THE PROBLEMS

After regularly attending the trustees' meetings, the consultants began to see areas where the trustees needed to
work. They had difficulty making decisions. Their meetings
were often long, frustrating, erratic, and disorderly. No one
seemed to listen or respond to what others said. No one was
able to build on previous contributions or acknowledge
when a decision had been made. The trustees and the rector
were also unable to decide about the rector's time away
from the parish for other activities, such as diocesan youth
work.

Being outsiders, the consultants were able to see the way

the trustees related to each other as persons and to point to some areas where they might improve their ways of arriving at decisions and working together. Because they were not directly involved in the meetings, the consultants could push the group to be clear and also make sure that the necessary follow-up actions were taken. In essence, they helped the trustees understand each other better. As one leader put it: "Martha and Harry got us to organize ourselves by asking questions like 'Who was going to do what?' This is something we should have done ten years ago and just didn't do it. They really helped us organize and look at ourselves with a more critical eye. We tried to figure out what we wanted to do, and they helped us do it."

Following the trustees' meetings, the consultant team met regularly with Dick Gilchrist to help him look at his style of leadership and how it affected the trustees. He was open and trusting, and he was able to receive feedback well, look at his behavior, and see ways to improve. Wanting very much for the vestry to take responsibility for the life of St. Bartholomew's and not wanting to be overdirective and dictatorial, he never expressed what he thought and felt. What he saw as making decisions by a general consensus, the consultants saw as abdication of leadership. Picking up on the consultants' observations, Gilchrist made a conscious decision to try new styles of leadership. He became freer to use more directive ways of leading in order to help the vestry work more effectively.

COMMUNICATIONS PROBLEMS ARISE

In an attempt to help the trustees learn to work more effectively together, the consultants designed a weekend away from the parish. On October 2, 1970, they gathered at a nearby farm. The first night, the group fantasized about their goals for St. Bartholomew's. They shared their dreams and then took a realistic look at their present state of affairs by reviewing the data of July 8 and 9, the feedback given to the rector, and the consultants' observations of their experiences so far.

Groups of three were formed to discuss the material. Two of these groups brought back substantial reports, but one group seemed unable to do the task. They reported back one comment: "Lack of humor." They went on to explain that they disliked the changes that were taking place in the Church in general. One member of that group passed around an article from *The Wall Street Journal* on the present-day troubles in the churches. Another felt negative about the consultants' work, stating that St. Bartholomew's had become too introspective and self-examining. As the total group discussed these comments, communication became confused and unproductive, some people getting defensive. The consultants were unable to free the members to communicate directly and clearly. The Board of Trustees adjourned for the night with the matter unresolved.

Reviewing the first night's events, both consultants saw the need to work on how members were relating and working together. They felt in a bind because several people involved in the communications breakdown were to be absent on Saturday. They therefore decided not to have trustees who would be present spend the time working on relationships with each other.

At the final sessions on Saturday morning the trustees tried to review how the church was organized, what their financial policies were, and their long-range goals. They made one concrete and satisfying decision—to assign one of the trustees to each parish committee to act as a liaison person to the board. The session otherwise proved to be very frustrating. Although the trustees were not working effectively together, every person present was able to see that they were unfree and needed to work on interpersonal relationships and communications. The consultants described the experience: "The whole atmosphere of the vestry was so oppressive at this point that nobody wanted to be there. It was as if they had run the mile and lost, and they knew they had to run it again. We could not conceive of the group having fun together. They disliked the things they knew about each other."

By mid-November, the working committees from the July parish planning sessions had thought through their list of concerns and had begun to take steps toward effective change. The consultants met all day on November 21 with the separate committees, reviewing their work and looking at future plans. They helped the group see what decisions and work still needed to be undertaken in order to reach their goals by the New Year, January 1, 1971.

A few days later, the consultant team attended a trustees' meeting and began renegotiating their working contract. Martha Adams observed that the meeting was very leaden. There were long periods of silence with little or no participation. The members were unresponsive to each other. The rector did not participate in the discussion and seemed unable to express his opinions clearly when called on to do so. Toward the end of the meeting, the board members began to discuss their own lack of effectiveness. Not one of them was pleased with the way they worked as a group, and they began to verbalize this to each other. The trustees generally accepted the consultants' proposals to continue their consultation, everyone agreeing that the trustees needed to work on their communications problems.

WORKING ON FREEING UP COMMUNICATIONS

In February 1971, the consultants held a team-building conference to help the trustees communicate and work more effectively together. Ten days prior to the weekend, Harry Pritchett and Martha Adams interviewed the rector and every trustee. Each person was asked to comment on the effectiveness of the board as a team and on the effectiveness of each trustee as a team member. The information was read back to each member and initialed by him or her. The member's comments and ideas would be shared with other trustees, but would not include his or her name.

At the first session each person read the collected interview material. The trustees responded to it by first making general comments, then giving more specific comments to individuals. Some of the issues dealt with were: the influence or power of some members, the leadership style of the vicar, the whole issue of support for each other. Several vestrymen seemed to change their behavior immediately after reading what others had said about them. One commented, "It's amazing! These folks really know me." A quieter member who learned that the others wanted to hear more from her began to speak up. The first night ended with a social gathering, some members continuing their conversations, others singing with a guitarist.

The changes from the interviews were reinforced the following morning by exploring the way decisions were made by the trustees. This discussion centered on the issues from the night before. Their general learnings were tested out during a business meeting in the afternoon. There was real sensitivity to listening to others and to hearing others out.

The consultants observed a great deal of leveling, openness, nondefensiveness, and support for each other as Board of Trustees members and as persons. There was a sense of caring about each member of the team as a real live human being with feelings, ambiguities, and resources.

During the evaluation, the trustees began to label what they had learned on the weekend. They felt the board was much more effective and operated in a more collaborative way than it had in the past. They began to make plans about the future of the parish. The consultants sensed a missionary zeal to carry to the rest of St. Bartholomew's members the kind of love, concern, and ability to work with each other that the trustees had discovered.

Their growth had not been without struggle and pain. As one board member reflected months later: "That was the first of the highlights. It was confronting and supportive. Nobody was untouched by it. I would recommend it every year." Another put it this way: "The PTP project brought us to the threshold of where the Holy Spirit is. We forced our needs to come out. We were obliged to resolve our interpersonal differences. We need to have the February event every year."

CLOSING THE CONSULTATION

In the spring of 1971, the Board of Trustees made a decision to postpone a conference that the consultants had proposed for the entire church. Dick Gilchrist, reporting the board's feelings to the consultants, assessed the situation as follows:

St. Bart's is beginning to read its own data and, we think, pretty accurately. People here are tired. They have really put out fantastically, I feel, and are now ready for some kind of creative breather. There also seems to be some resistance to "PTP," which I think is healthy. There is the desire to do some digging on our own and see what, if any, real significant contribution "we" can do here alone. It is also the "winding down" part of the year. Hence, no major conference as we had proposed. A year ago the board would have gone ahead halfheartedly out of duty, and would have attempted to have the conference. But now they can say, "No," and not feel bad about it. I think this is honest and has some broad implications in regard to accountability.

Gilchrist went on to write of his personal feelings about the parish and his ministry:

I have never felt better at St. Bartholomew's than I do now. I feel more free, more open, and more relaxed than ever before. It started after the team-building and has been going on ever since, even with the *crush* of Easter, income tax, camp coming up, etc., etc. I feel good about being here and, contrary to some of the things I said at team-building (vestry meetings are "I-them"), many of these things have changed. This may be an illusion—but people seem more responsive to me, too.

In August, the Board of Trustees voted to postpone a decision about future consultation until the fall. One vestry-woman described the session as having a layer of tension: "There was a general feeling that we had done all we could do and we didn't want to spend any more money. I felt dissatisfied because most people wanted to say, 'let's quit,' but did not say it. We were tired."

Finally, in the fall, the consultant team met with the board to get a "yes" or "no" decision. They were asked to conclude the consultation by helping with the Every Member Canvass. Because of the strong rapport between the trustees and the consultants, a final decision was difficult. Both parties had entered an intense relationship, often frustrating but often rewarding. Harry Pritchett and Martha Adams had invested a great deal in St. Bartholomew's and the church had responded with trust and affection.

Although the team did not provide consultative help on financial matters until the end of their consultation, pledged income increased 31 per cent in the two years—10 per cent in 1971 and 21 per cent for 1972. The consultants attribute this to greater satisfaction in parish life rather than to increase in membership. Their membership has remained about the same; six new families have joined, while six have moved out of town.

Although the consultation was terminated with the Every Member Canvass in November 1971, St. Bartholomew's growth and learnings about new ways to operate continue to be used. Dick Gilchrist, wanting to reinforce the process that has been started, sees his role evolving as that of an internal consultant to the parish. Parishioners still have concerns and issues they continue to work on. The parish committees on evangelism and outreach have merged and are struggling to find answers appropriate to St. Bartholomew's.

Just as parishioners at St. Bartholomew's have felt their lives being creatively stretched, so others see the growth of the parish. The Rev. James Thompson, a Presbyterian minister from a nearby church, comments on the change in attitudes at St. Bartholomew's since the consultation:

It's not that they are doing different things—they were always very involved—but they understand better what they are about. There is a growing sense of openness. They are able to participate in projects without insisting on their own terms. PTP seems to have helped them find their own identity. They had been worrying about their small size. They seem to have discovered a sense of autonomy or growth which has gone beyond the issue of numerical strength. Dick also has grown. He came here open and caring, but he has grown in his ability to plan his own role and evaluate himself. Part of what has been going on during consultation has spilled over into my work at Westminster as we have been doing similar things. It has been supportive to us. I think I can say with some degree of certainty that outside consultation has accelerated the process of "getting it together" because I have tried to do the same things alone and haven't had it happen as well or as fast.

CONCLUSION

The story of St. Bartholomew's is not that of a dying parish experiencing a dramatic revival. Rather, it is the story of a group of committed people working together and developing ways to make their life more satisfying. One parishioner describes the changes like this: "Before the consultation we were at a low ebb. Five families had moved away and money was down. We had started, but had not moved off dead center. We were floundering. PTP gave us confidence to find the human resources and talent in the people that the congregation had."

St. Bartholomew's experience can best be seen in terms of freedom—freedom from frustrations that inhibit satisfaction and joy, and freedom for new life, creative and threatening. By freeing themselves from organizational inefficiency, the parishioners became able to see their interpersonal shortcomings. As they found new life in relating to one another, they grew more secure about who they were as a congregation. No longer feeling like a "colony" of Trinity Church, St. Bartholomew's began asking questions about what its unique mission was. The people there are seriously working on the meaning of their Good News. To develop an ongoing process of working together, of questioning their life and purpose, of wrestling with their own mission—this is what "The Story of St. Bartholomew's" is all about.

E.L.D.

$$4$$

THE STORY OF
FIRST CHURCH

A CHURCH IN CONFLICT

On the corner of Fourth and South Kline in Aberdeen, South Dakota, stands First United Presbyterian Church. Some call this Gothic church with its huge sanctuary and stained-glass windows "the most beautiful building in the city." Others find it a bit dark and forbidding. It has about nine hundred members, many of them well-to-do, leading citizens of Aberdeen, which is a bustling shopping area serving extensive farmlands around it. Many of the members are retired farmers, strong people and rugged individualists.

In the summer of 1970, the minister of First Church left after years of mounting tension with the leaders of the church. A large number of members, including many who had appreciated his pastoral care in sickness and bereavement, were angry, feeling the pastor had been "run out." But a number of the leaders were relieved he had finally gone. The presbytery[1] had first tried to help the minister

[1] The presbytery is the corporate regional unit of the ministry of the Presbyterian Church.

and leaders communicate with each other, and then, finding this impossible, dissolved the relationship between minister and congregation. An Administrative Commission[2] was appointed to take responsibility for the parish until a new minister was found. In spite of the painful splits between supporters and opponents of the former pastor, between older and younger members of the church, between parish leaders and the rest of the congregation, the moderator of the commission could say, "I believe they are ready to enter into a period of intense searching that can move the church from an uncertain past to a meaningful future."

AN INTERIM MINISTER COMES TO FIRST CHURCH

The Rev. Keith Irwin, who was interested in combining the roles of consultant and interim pastor, was asked to come to Aberdeen for an interview with the Administrative Commission and then the Session.[3] Keith Irwin spoke to the Session members of his own "restlessness and unsatisfied feelings about many things in the institutional Church." He made it clear that he was not interested in just "baby-sitting" the church until a permanent minister could be found, but wanted to help the congregation look at its problems: "We could have lots of fun taking a good long evaluative look at the entire picture of the Aberdeen Church." The reaction the commission had feared—to "an expert from the East out here to tell us what to do"—did not take place. After the Session voted unanimously to ask Irwin to come to

[2] An Administrative Commission is sometimes appointed by a presbytery to assist a local congregation in dealing with difficult problems.

[3] The Session is the governing body of a local Presbyterian congregation.

Aberdeen in this dual role, people gathered around him to say, "I have new hope for this church," and, "I really look forward to what can happen."

Keith Irwin "comes on easy." He has a warm and accepting manner, and this communicates in his warm handclasp or, with old friends, his affectionate bear hug. His hair is gray, but his ability to try new ideas or new behavior mark him with an inner youthfulness. He laughs spontaneously when happy and looks miserable when he *is* miserable. There is an iron core to him, though, that is willing to press hard issues, confront difficult tasks or people directly, and stick to his guns when he feels it is important. He has deep empathy for others and is quickly sensitive to unspoken concerns. His wife Marian is his associate in every way. Sharing his warmth and empathic nature, she too has adaptability and willingness to try new ideas. For many years they have often led training conferences together, and the work in Aberdeen would be approached as a joint task. Marian Irwin's skills in group process, observation, and evaluation were to prove invaluable.

The idea of "contract" was foreign to the people at First Church, and Keith Irwin had to press them for a clear written agreement so that both he and they would have similar expectations of the special skills he would use and the special role he would play. The contract made it clear that he was not a "baby-sitter," but that he would be taking specific steps to help them identify their problems and begin working on them. The contract became an important element in the work at Aberdeen, supporting and clarifying the decisions Irwin made about work priorities.

Before moving to Aberdeen, Irwin also entered into a contract with this writer to provide full reports of his work to Project Test Pattern and to ask for or accept any consultation that either he or PTP felt would be helpful. Project Test Pattern would also provide further training and whatever other help it could. In its contract with Irwin, the parish agreed both to the absences from the parish that the training would make necessary and to help defray the costs of the consultation and training.

On December 10, 1970, Keith and Marian Irwin arrived in Aberdeen and were delighted to find the manse furnished, eggs, bacon, bread, and milk in the refrigerator, and even a Christmas tree already decorated. On the first Sunday, at a reception held for the Irwins, Keith explained to the congregation the double role he would be trying to fulfill. He put on the table an old, comfortable hiking shoe to symbolize the role of the pastor, who would do traditional and expected things like preaching, baptizing, burying. A new black dress shoe on the table stood for that part of his role which would be new and different and might be uncomfortable.

In Session meetings that night and in following days, it became clear that the congregation was, indeed, angry and split. Some people were withholding pledges in anger about the previous minister, and the Trustees[4] were tense about budget deficits. Members of the staff felt that they were expected to carry heavy loads of work, but that they got little appreciation or emotional support.

FINDING THE PROBLEMS

Keith and Marian Irwin began visiting families at once to find out and write down as much as they could about the

---

[4] The Trustees manage the financial affairs of the local Presbyterian congregation.

problems in the parish. People had been aware of the contract; they understood that the Irwins were not just making
routine pastoral calls, but were gathering information to
help the congregation identify its own problems. As Irwin
met with individuals and groups over the next two months,
he began to learn more about what was wrong at First
Church. "I feel members do not really know or appreciate
one another as persons. . . . There isn't much evidence of
satisfaction in being involved in church tasks." Session
members said, "I was never so glad as when I got off the
Session!" The Session was unclear about its goals and responsibilities, and tended to leave most jobs to the staff.
People in the community and the presbytery saw it as a
church with strength and with problems. Some made these
comments: "First Church has a tradition of being a 'strong
pulpit' church. Yet it is a church with a history of being
rough on its ministers. . . . There is a weakness in the
church which depends on a 'strong pulpit.' There tends to
be too much dependence on the minister, or the opposite,
rebellion at his authority." "Much energy has been dissi-
pated in conflict when utilization of conflict can be energy
releasing . . . not much life or energy flows outward to
community or world."

Young people were bored. At one youth group meeting
Irwin attended he found that the "kids were just lumps. The
kids do not seem to be in charge of their own thing at all."
In church on Sunday, people were sitting in scattered, separated groups. "There is a large balcony in the rear over the
narthex," Irwin explained. "A lot of people choose to sit up
there. There are lots of vacant pews near the front of the
sanctuary. An attempt was made more than once to shut off
the balcony and force people to come down. A loud wailing
cry was heard!" The physical separation dramatized the

way people were cut off from each other. "In general," he concluded, "I see this whole congregation as needing a lot of hearty love."

WORKING ON THE FINDINGS

Because he was the interim minister as well as a consultant, Mr. Irwin was able to use traditional pastoral functions to begin to speak to the problems he was discovering. In his sermons he spoke about "the joy-bringing possibilities of being *for* one another" in the midst of situations full of conflict; about "the possibility of really seeing a person"; about "paying some attention to the 'product' that church 'business' is supposed to produce." He made a decision to meet with parishioners after services to get feedback on the sermons, to try to break through the pattern of the minister having all the answers. He had never done this before and felt anxious about it, particularly the first time. Some genuine dialogue developed.

During a training program in Washington, D.C., Keith Irwin met with me to talk about how members of the congregation could begin to make the information he had been gathering from them their own. Back in Aberdeen, he worked out with the Session a series of six Lenten potluck supper meetings to explore the six major problem areas he had discovered in his visits with parish families. Leaders for these meetings were given some training in human relations and working with groups. This training, Irwin reported later, "was a most enjoyable time for us—to see how very hungry people are just to *be* and just to *meet*! . . . What I most hoped would happen did happen: that these very dear and gifted people would get just a whiff of how everyone has been having only surface contact with each other. And that this is one of the great reasons for joylessness in the church."

The trained leaders (Irwin had to be away) began the Lenten series with a discussion of "Goals and Aspirations" —what was the church supposed to do? People stayed around talking until 10 P.M., a departure from their usual practice of leaving immediately after scheduled meetings. A summary of the groups' findings was passed around the next Wednesday, when they went on to talk about the issue of "Communication"—how open, free, and sensitive are people at First Church? Irwin wrote in his report on this evening: "One kind of change that seems more and more visible is in the degree of speaking up and out even on conflicting opinions. Another, awareness that people are getting acquainted with each other."

The Wednesday night discussion of "Destructive Behavior Patterns" came up with a list of one hundred fifty-nine kinds of behavior that hurt individuals and the community. The following week, groups worked on the issue of "Church Structures"—to carry out goals.

The tension of the pastor/consultant double role was reflected in Irwin's reports of his work, particularly at this time, in March, after four months in Aberdeen. He reported that he felt tired, uncertain, and restless, "with the feeling that I am being drawn into the busy, busywork of a parish, doing a lot of things which add up to nothing. People like us and seem to appreciate what we are trying to do. But I have the feeling that no one really is very much interested in any changes."

On the fifth Lenten evening, each group was given old magazines, colored paper, sticks, etc., and asked to make a collage showing what they wanted to say about the church.

Leaders observed the process of the group—what happened between the people as they worked—and then talked with the members about what they had seen.

The last session dealt with "Rewards and Satisfactions." Can life in the church be fulfilling? Can people's level of satisfaction be an index of the health of the church?

On Easter, a sunrise agape meal was planned and led entirely by ninth and tenth graders, and at the later service more than five hundred people filled the church. Although the Easter services were a high point, and although there were a number of signs that there was more openness and less conflict in the congregation, Irwin continued to wonder how far the church had come: "I am at present sort of depressed at the potentialities of this congregation, which seem so far from being actualized. I have heard the Lord say to me on numerous occasions, 'PATIENCE, JACKASS!' "

A weekend retreat for parish leaders on April 30 moved forward with the information about problems that had been gathered from and worked on by the congregation in Lent. These four urgent priorities were set: (1) spiritual kindling or rekindling, (2) improved human relations, (3) leadership training, (4) Christian education. During the retreat and follow-up meetings, some specific plans were made to work on these priorities.

LOOKING FOR A NEW MINISTER

In the midst of the retreat, the Pastor-Seeking Committee had its third meeting. In the United Presbyterian Church the work of this committee is demanding and complicated. It must fill out lengthy forms carefully analyzing what the congregation is, what it needs to become, and what it sees

the role of the pastor to be. The committee had been participating in this analysis along with the whole congregation, as
it sought to identify and work on parish problems.

In its reports, the Pastor-Seeking Committee accepted responsibility for the way previous ministers had been treated:
"It is obvious that in the past we have made the minister
feel high, dry, lonesome, and frustrated." The committee
felt it was important to be honest with any prospective pastor about how far the congregation still had to go in developing strong lay leadership and how much they wanted him
to help train these leaders. "What does it mean for a congregation to be good to a minister? Well, for one thing, it
means to spell out what the congregation is really after. It
means to provide him with clear goals to work toward."
One member summed up how far the church had come
since the previous summer: "If we had gone right to another
pastor immediately after [the former minister left], it would
have been a disaster." Keith Irwin's reaction to the report
was: "I have never heard such clear, concise statements.
They served to wipe away all the fears I had."

The contract had been kept by the people, as well as by
the interim pastor, and they were ready to enter into a clear
and honest covenant with a new minister.

LEAVING ABERDEEN

In the middle of May, the high school graduates were
honored at Sunday morning worship. Keith Irwin reported:
"I asked the congregation, during the closing hymn, to move
down to the front and gather around the seniors as they
stood in front of the Communion Table—as a sign of our
being with them. The congregation did respond, and it was
a moving experience for everyone." People hugged each

other. A man who was there said, "He gave us a freedom."
The congregation which had earlier expressed the character
of its corporate life by sitting in little islands was now able
to move together in an act of support.

Two more leadership training sessions were held by Keith
Irwin, and "a laboratory experience in human communica-
tion" was planned for September, before he and his wife left
Aberdeen on June 16.

At the laboratory at Blue Cloud Abbey many deep feelings were openly shared. The weekend ended with an agape
feast which Irwin described as follows:

The wine and a small loaf were placed on the round coffee table
in the midst of the group. On our feet, in a circle, we passed the
peace—and this was done with touching, with hugs, with the kiss
of peace. Many already were in tears. Then, people served each
other around the circle. . . . In the main, what was lifted up was
the new awareness of the capacity each had for love—to give, and
to receive. And now that some of the things that block the flow
have gotten out of the way, there can be this very sincere love.

On July 9, Robert Macfarlane of the Division of Evangelism of the United Presbyterian Church, went with me to
Aberdeen to spend a day interviewing members of First
Church about the period of Keith Irwin's interim ministry/
consultation. In several cases individuals or groups were
given copies of the contract and were asked to use it to evaluate the interim pastorate. In one interview group I began
the discussion by asking, "Well, how are things going?"
There was silence. Then one trustee said, "One change is
nobody's holding back on pledges anymore!" The group's
laughter was immediate, testifying to their relief about this
particular bit of evidence of a tangible change in their congregation.

In my report of that visit, I said, "Irwin's work was identified as having two major levels—the data-gathering, analysis, feedback level leading to the statement the congregation developed about where it is and what it needs in a new minister; and the climate-changing level which will (it is hoped) make the congregation more ready to respond and support the minister who is called." "The outside person," said one member, "can see things those in the community take for granted."

People felt communication had been improved, barriers had been broken down, conflict could be dealt with. People could care about each other. Said one young member, "He made me more open. In fact, I'm so open now it scares me."

One member, a dentist, said, "There was a big difference in the attitude of the congregation after Keith. More friendliness, love. . . . Three weeks ago when I went to the service I waved at a guy who never speaks to me, and he looked away. The next Sunday I put my arm around him, and he sort of smiled. The next week, he waved at me!" Keith Irwin's affectionate reaching out had been contagious, and the dentist had been enabled to risk trying something very new at First Church.

It became clear that "there was an increase in understanding of the need of any minister for effective support from the congregation and an increased awareness of the possibility of a pastor-laity team for ministering." Macfarlane and I observed that the Session was operating as an effective leadership team and showed little evidence of the divisions that had existed eight months earlier.

There were ambivalences. There were feelings that Keith Irwin had left too soon, and feelings that the congregation should not move too far on its own until it had a "permanent" pastor.

Looking forward to the possibility of another interim pastor/consultant job, Keith Irwin reflected in his dossier his own conception of ministry: "To bring about maximum growth and fulfillment of lives; to help each other deal with crippling hang-ups which block the flow of human love."

L. B. M. with C E L I A A. H A H N

THE STORY OF ST. MARK'S

It was a dark, windy Whitsunday at St. Mark's Church. The church school had been getting ready for its last day by making bright banners to carry, along with red balloons, out the church door for the annual Whitsunday parade around Capitol Hill in Washington, D.C. The congregation gathered around the central altar was greeted with a bombshell. The Speaker of the House had just proposed that four blocks, including St. Mark's Church, be razed to make way for an addition to the Library of Congress. "I still cannot imagine the total destruction of its unique, graceful Romanesque arches or its brilliant windows, or its high-beamed ceiling which has sheltered our laughter, our drinking and dancing, as well as our tears and tragedies and worship of our Lord God," said the rector, the Rev. James Adams, in his sermon. The church's birthday party parade quickly became a protest march. Angry and fearful for their church, yet stimulated and united by the need to act, people started writing "Save St. Mark's" messages to attach to the helium-filled balloons. Feelings were high as the congregation trooped out the

church doors at the end of the service, and let go of the red
balloons. Some balloons got caught in the trees, but gusts of
wind blew others toward the House office buildings.

St. Mark's has something to save. It has taken a seven-teen-year trip from the verge of death to life.

St. Mark's Church is an old urban parish, set in a rapidly changing neighborhood. The building is within walking distance of the nation's Capitol and Union Station. The Library of Congress and the Supreme Court are St. Mark's closest neighbors, along with interracial slums, small businesses, and expensively restored houses. Diversity and contrast are everywhere. "The Hill" houses both young and old, rich and poor, black and white, educated and uneducated.

In 1954, suffering troubled days in a changing neighborhood, St. Mark's was a dying church. The Rt. Rev. Angus Dun, then Bishop of Washington, saw no hope for the parish, and suggested that an elderly priest be named rector, so that at his retirement the doors which closed on him would also close on St. Mark's. The vestry firmly rejected the idea. Some younger members of the parish made a dramatic decision to remain on Capitol Hill and minister to its residents regardless of their diversity in property, profession, skill, or color. The Rev. William M. Baxter was called to lead the way to that future for St. Mark's. A flyer addressed to "Interested Pagans, Bored Christians, Others" was typical of early efforts to reach out into the neighborhood.

St. Mark's began an intensive task of examining its reason for being and keeping its buildings open. Mr. Baxter, described by those who know him as a charismatic clergyman, is very emphatic about his style of ministry and what it means to him. He is convinced that the importance of Chris-

tianity can best be understood through a personal experience of judgment and redemption within the framework of
a holy community. He sees his function as helping a congregation experience the depth of the holy on the human scene.

A vivid way of experiencing a slice of life in the midst of
the holy community, and then reflecting on it, was provided
through chancel drama. St. Mark's founded a theatrical
group, the Washington Chancel Drama Cycle, which presented more than four hundred fifty performances of sixty-
five plays over a ten-year period in twenty-two different
churches. Each performance was followed by a discussion in
which people were encouraged to talk about the issues in
their lives that were raised by the play. A willingness to
bring all phases of life into the church itself is still a very
central part of the "St. Mark's Experience."

A CONSULTANT IN EDUCATION

Feeling that he wanted to make Christian education central and that he needed to work as part of a team, Bill Baxter had already secured the services of Lilly Kester as
trainee in Christian education. In 1955 he raised $2,500 to
bring in an educational consultant, Dr. Charles Penniman,
Director of the Educational Center in St. Louis. With the
help of Dr. Penniman, St. Mark's began an educational program based on the Educational Center's rationale: that the
real issue of life is the tension between sin and faith; that
with careful supervision a climate can be created whereby a
person can touch the despair and tragedy of his or her own
life and come to terms with what undergirds his or her per-
sonhood.

The educational program at St. Mark's became the foun-
dation and reason for the existence of the parish. In describ-

ing his commitment to this strategy, Baxter explained that the more a parishioner became involved in the educational program, the more aware he or she became that all other aspects flow through that one function: pastoral life, worship, administration, mission, and social concerns. Education went on everywhere at St. Mark's, and it remains the highest priority for the congregation. As described in the "Parish Brochure" of 1959: "St. Mark's makes serious demands upon people inquiring about Christianity and those who seek communicant membership in this church."

In 1962, eight years after Dr. Penniman began consulting with the parish, Mrs. Harriet Gregory was hired as a full-time Director of Christian Education. She devoted her energies to developing a core of lay people who could teach other lay people, using theological categories and symbolic reflections with precision. She was responsible for the supervision of the program—reading, annotating, and evaluating volumes of transcriptions from the individual classes.

The church school had been strengthened in morale and organization during Lilly Kester's years at St. Mark's. It was important not only for nurture of children in the meaning of contemporary faith and real life, but because it provided an arena for the training of adult leadership in understanding the philosophy of education at St. Mark's. According to Bill Baxter:

Children and adults learned in the classroom setting not by discussing life in general, but only in conversation when life was under some sort of pressure: a decision to be made, a problem to be faced. A person only talked about religion when the pressure was on from the outside, when commitments were in conflict. Under these conditions, it was possible to discover what really motivated a person, where one's ultimate values lay. In this experience,

Christian symbols might be mirrors to see the situation more clearly. The class lived an experience instead of talking about it.

The Rev. James Adams, the present rector, has described how Penniman's theory is carried out as a class moves through a series of deepening levels of experience:

1. Being curious

The class members find themselves and one another in a problem, such as the tension between group responsibility and personal independence.

2. Being anxious

As they get in touch with the contradictory pressures within each person, the class members become increasingly uneasy.

3. Hoping

The discovery that they are all anxious beneath their social facades gives them a common bond and a sense of joy that they can face the worst in themselves and bear it.

4. Despairing

Inevitably the class members move away from their creative insights and determination to be honest and realistic.

5. Anticipating

In the final stage, the members of the class come to terms with their despair about themselves and discover a sense of community which can provide a constant reminder of their discoveries.

Jim Adams sees the educational process as a discipline, rather than an educational theory. From his point of view, the results of this approach to education were amazing:

I discovered to my great joy that the people who had been through an adult education class which helped make some sense out of their lives were often eager to continue their education by becoming teachers themselves. I have never had any problems getting teachers when I could assure them of a partner and regular supervision for their work. In fact, I have a serious problem of not being able to place all the volunteers.

The qualification for church school teaching is a willingness to be honest—with the supervisor, the class, and oneself— and to work within the discipline.

AN ARCHITECT AS CONSULTANT

As St. Mark's life became increasingly vital, the people became more aware of the limitations of the physical structure. The acoustics were poor in the parish hall, and there was no other place to meet in small groups. In the spring of 1965 Kent Cooper and Associates, an architectural firm in Washington, was hired to conduct an intensive master-planning program. The purpose was to make the existing building more functional for the specific programs and activities involved in parish life at St. Mark's. Under the leadership of Mr. Cooper (who had also been influenced by the work of Dr. Penniman), the architectural committee, including the rector, education director, and twelve parishioners, was taken through a strenuous process of self-study and evaluation.

Committee members began work by evaluating the existing church structures and studying parish programs. Early in the process two themes were clearly identified. The first concerned the climate: St. Mark's was characterized by an adventurous spirit of experiment and new life, and by a willingness to become involved. The second was that their existing church structure was a landmark worth preserving and enhancing. From these two themes the major issue for St. Mark's was discovered: "Does this landmark adequately support the new life which has been found and carefully nurtured here?" The architectural committee began to realize that in many respects the current programs succeeded despite the existing building, not because of it.

In Kent Cooper's initial letter to the architectural committee, he explained what he would be searching for from the group. The committee needed to uncover "that unutterable secret by which they secure their identity." Explaining the work of the architectural committee, Bill Baxter wrote:

We wanted to do something that would make the building support and enhance "faith working through love" (Gal. 5:6). One part of this is keeping faith with the past and with those who, to the best of their knowledge and commitment, have sheltered us and given us St. Mark's. Now we must carry our inherited responsibility into the present age, into the now, for the young, for those who need Christ most desperately—the Christ who is seen in faith working through love. I feel that a church, even more than a home, should be a very special place of birth, a place of special understanding of death. St. Mark's should be a place where one is moved between them by the very presence of loving care. This is what our building plans are all about.

While the bricks inside the church were scrubbed and the pillars painted, the pews were taken out, and the congregation met in the parish hall for worship around a central altar. When the time came to move back, the people were so satisfied with this arrangement that they sold the pews and surrounded the altar with chairs on four sides. The chairs and altar could be moved, and the church itself used for small group discussions, dances, and other parish programs, as well as worship. All of the church's life could be lived and lifted up in the holy place.

Life is very much present in worship at St. Mark's. Sunday morning services are carefully planned by rector and lay people to focus on and lift up the deepest concerns of the people. The coming together of the community is a central and vital action, often dramatic and deeply moving.

A NEW RECTOR

In 1966, after twelve years at St. Mark's, Bill Baxter resigned his position as rector to work as a director for the Peace Corps in Washington, and the Rev. James R. Adams became rector of St. Mark's. Although Jim Adams' basic philosophy was similar to that of his predecessor, he brought with him a new style of leadership and a new set of abilities. His constant honesty, nondefensive stance, and personal discipline inspire his friends to describe him as "rigidly open." Adams made some basic changes in the structure of the staff. Harriet Gregory's title was changed to Consultant in Education, and her responsibilities were renegotiated so that she taught selected adults and trained supervisors. Since the entire educational program was built on the system of consultants, the training of supervisors was of primary importance.

Shortly after he arrived in 1966, Jim Adams led the vestry on what was to become an annual weekend retreat, to make plans for the coming year. The rector and vestry worked out parish policies for specific areas, such as baptism, confirmation, funerals, and marriages. The group also wrote some statements of identity for St. Mark's. Some members called this their battle cry:

St. Mark's is where the good news of freedom (to be human, to be right, to be wrong, from the law, to be judged) and forgiveness given by Jesus Christ is projected by the life of the community and hopefully heard. This is not something that can be told. Only through involvement can one appropriate it. This is not a prescription for your life, but an invitation to join.

St. Mark's is a community whose purpose is to nurture and support its people in discovering who they are and where they are. Church is primarily a training camp (discovering with others where the battles are and equipping me for the fight), not an operating combat unit.

Church gives me courage to be who I am. Church is to do for others what it did for me. Honesty—openness—makes life better but more difficult. St. Mark's is unique. Coffee hour is like a rally after a football game where we won.

After the first few months of Mr. Adams' ministry at St. Mark's, he began to get indications from the congregation that their life together was not moving smoothly. He had numerous complaints that his sermons sounded like lectures. During a Sunday morning service in December, Jim Adams turned over the sermon time for a discussion. The congregation was highly critical of his sermons. As Jim described it: "They ripped me to shreds."

While willing to profit from the criticisms, he felt that there was more to this problem than merely the quality of his sermons. It was his suspicion that the congregation had not adequately dealt with Mr. Baxter's leaving, and he

asked Bill Baxter to come back for a sermon discussion on a
Sunday morning so that the congregation could settle its un-
finished business with him. At that discussion, many members expressed anger with Baxter for resigning. They expressed feelings of rejection and desertion, of grief and loss.
Over the years Bill Baxter had developed strong personal
ties with the congregation which made the adjustment to a
new rector very difficult. After their strong feelings were
aired and talked about with him, the members of the congregation were better able to allow Jim Adams to become
their rector.

A PSYCHIATRIC CONSULTANT

Bill Baxter had secured the services of Dr. Maxwell Boverman, a psychiatrist in private practice in Washington, as
consultant. With Boverman's help, Baxter came to realize
the disproportionate amount of time he had been spending
with some parishioners who continued to come to him with
their problems while refusing to give any heed to his coun-
sel. Dr. Boverman helped him realize the inordinate toll he
was paying in angry and depleted feelings by continuing in
these futile relationships and also helped him release himself
from them.

Together they developed a team approach to people in
trouble. Baxter was often included in therapy sessions, and,
as a clergyman, was free to go to the patient's home, to raise
questions and press for action in a way that would be inappropriate for Dr. Boverman.

After Jim Adams (who had also worked with Boverman in
his previous parish) came to St. Mark's, an incident of suicide occurred which shocked the parish community. Rather
than minister to each parishioner individually, Adams and

Boverman decided to treat the entire congregation as a family in grief. A traditional funeral with Eucharist helped the bereaved family and the congregation act out their grief. The next Sunday the service was designed to help the members begin to resolve their painful feelings. Jim Adams shared his own feelings:

The first question I raised was, "Why did he do it?" I cited some possible reasons and pointed to some learnings we could make. I also talked about my own feelings of failure, grief, and anger. I felt some satisfaction by explaining how the Church in the Middle Ages treated suicide—by damning the person and burying him at the crossroads. I concluded by pointing to our task. We could never know the truth about the deceased, but we had to know what was happening to us, so we could be free to move on. The truth could set us free.

After the service, any person who wanted to was invited to stay and talk about the experience. Mr. Adams led the discussion while Dr. Boverman acted as consultant to the parishioners—helping them to identify their feelings and to focus on the real issues in their own lives. Dr. Boverman described the work of the group in the following way:

Parishioners began to face their feelings of irrational guilt, associated with suppressed anger and their fantasies about what caused the death. They were able to expose their attempted use of scapegoatism in order to avoid grief and blame. By realizing their irrational guilt, something beneficial was resolved. There seemed to be a sense of calmness and composure within the group.

The parish was soon confronted again with the issue of life and death. In February 1970, Harriet Gregory discovered that she had terminal cancer. She remained active in the educational program as long as she was physically able to do so, and she attended church even longer. On Whitsunday, her last Sunday, she was carried into church on a cot. Jim Adams spoke in his sermon about Harriet Gregory, about the troubled times he had experienced with her, and about the pressures and difficulties she had faced in the educational program. He spoke of her as the custodian of a tradition, as the symbol of an approach to education, and as a woman who had held a priestly role at St. Mark's. Mrs. Gregory died a few weeks later, and her funeral was held at the 11 o'clock service on Sunday morning. Three people who had known her well spoke briefly in tribute to her. Jim Adams feels that her burial service at the weekly congregational gathering was itself a personal tribute and an affirmation of her educational commitment—a discipline based on facing life's situations.

A VARIETY OF OUTSIDE RESOURCES

The use of outside consultants is standard procedure at St. Mark's. Jim Adams feels that the most important professional discovery he has made is that he needs help to do his job effectively. He attributes his positive experiences in the parish ministry to the use of outside consultants to help the parish realize its potential.

In 1967, though things seemed to be running smoothly, Jim Adams' morale was low. He was feeling exploited and resentful. A six-week program, entitled "What Kind of Help Helps?" and led by psychologist Donald S. Jewel, brought some light. A continuing theme that presented itself in the sessions was the idea that to be a helper, one had to be appreciated. Participants began to see that while people at St. Mark's were experts in dealing with anger, grief, and other strong negative feelings, they found it hard to express appreciation and warmth.

In 1968, during parish planning conferences led by diocesan consultants John C. Harris and James D. Anderson, analogous learnings took place. Though many responses by parishioners to the question, "What would make life in this parish more rewarding for me?" seemed negative and critical, the consultants helped the parishioners see that they were really hungry for more significant participation. The real meaning of the critical comments was, "We need more ways to express our commitments." The St. Mark's vestry began addressing the request for more involvement from parishioners by working toward more participatory worship services. A plan was also developed to have the congregation review and evaluate specific parish functions.

The following year the vestry conference, with the help of Mr. Timothy Murray, an industrial management consultant, moved on to implement this deeper participation and involvement. The policy statement which came out of the weekend's work included the following description of St. Mark's:

St. Mark's has helped each of us as individuals to discover the courage and freedom to act responsibly toward each other and toward the larger community. We have recognized the risk and pain involved in taking a stand. Acting corporately as a church in relation to the community, St. Mark's will be drawn into the tragic realities which afflict the society and which draw us into judgment on a personal level. Yet in finding a capacity to act in faith, it is our hope to be a witness to the strength found through Christ's people.

Specific funds were budgeted for community concerns.

In 1970, the Rev. James C. Fenhagen, rector of St. John's Episcopal Church, Georgetown, was hired as consultant for the vestry conference. As the weekend progressed, Mr. Fenhagen shared with the group his observation that the participants seemed very uncomfortable using words like "God" and "Jesus Christ." The "God" issue was not an easy one for the vestry, yet they were able to begin working on what this resistance meant and how they were going to overcome their uncomfortable feelings. In September an adult class called "The God Seminar" met to discuss theology. Gradually some members of the congregation grew to feel more comfortable with the transcendent dimension of their faith.

During this year, St. Mark's continuing concern for a social ministry had become more intense. On three days in June, after the vestry conference, a third of the active members participated in a Racism Institute, sponsored by the Metropolitan Ecumenical Training Center of Washington, D.C. As a result of the serious work done by the participants, St. Mark's[1] became more aware of the subtle ways it exhibited racist attitudes, both in individual life and as an institution.

St. Mark's Church made a determined commitment to demonstrate clearly its awareness of the race problem and its willingness to act on its beliefs. As an outgrowth of the Racism Institute, St. Mark's was increasingly making its facilities available to neighborhood groups and supporting community group projects and businesses with both money and time. Studies were underway to inform parishioners where their individual savings deposits could support the

[1] In St. Mark's congregation of two hundred two members, sixteen members are black, including the present senior warden, who is a woman.

community welfare and where discrimination was an apparent institutional policy. Discussions were being conducted with other churches and black groups to determine how opportunities for greater interaction and communication between the races could be fostered. Ten per cent of the church budget for 1971 was allocated to community action. The group also suggested steps to be taken by members of segregated clubs. There was general agreement that St. Mark's clergy would increase their community involvement.

IDENTITY AND LEADERSHIP

A brief summary of the character of St. Mark's would focus on sense of identity and style of leadership.

St. Mark's has a dynamic and self-conscious sense of identity. Who are we? Where are we? Where are we going? These questions are constantly asked and grappled with as deeply and honestly as possible. St. Mark's is an intense place. A high priority is placed on the ability to confront one another, to be honest. Facing negative feelings—despair, conflict, guilt—and dealing with them is seen as a primary responsibility, and as the gateway to joy. Those who couldn't take the intensity and the spotlight on painful feelings have dropped out. St. Mark's members had to be pushed toward learning to express affection toward each other and to feel comfortable with positive traditional symbols.

The commitment of St. Mark's members to their church is intense. The way in is a demanding confirmation class, and the way out is a parting ritual in which departing members give their reasons for leaving. One evidence of this intense commitment is the fact that St. Mark's has one of the highest per capita giving records in the diocese.

The architecture expresses the intensity. All of the church's life is to be lived and looked at honestly, as a drama represented in front of the altar.

St. Mark's continues to see the education program, with its emphasis on disciplined preparation and "homework," as the center of its life. What turns on St. Mark's members is the idea of church as "training camp," not "an operating combat unit" moving out to fight the world's battles. But, paradoxically, though "moving out" is not central to St. Mark's sense of identity, it is happening. Dealing with the deep realities of people's lives prepares St. Mark's members to say, "Church is to do for others what it did for me."

St. Mark's could not be the unique parish it is today without the strong and richly varied leadership it has had. Both rectors provided the congregation with firm guidance and direction. Each clergyman not only had clearly developed his own strongly personal style of leadership, but was aware of the power he had to influence the congregation. Each had a willingness and a commitment to continue the parish's change efforts over a long period of time.

The strength of the clerical leadership did not overshadow, but rather enhanced the growth in leadership on the part of the laity. The functional approach to education raised strong and capable lay leadership. Parishioners knew that St. Mark's was their parish and that they were responsible for it. The congregation learned to pay serious attention to the issues in the life of a church, developing a strong determination to work on an issue until it was resolved. Through their persistence, the members learned to take power over their own lives and the life of their congregation.

More unusual than the reliance on clergy and lay leadership has been St. Mark's continual use of outside consultants and resources. Many parishes use architects, but few find ways of using the architectural consultant to deepen and express the church's identity. Many clergy are in touch with psychiatric consultants, but few have found ways of linking that consultation to broad pastoral issues. Many parishes use educational innovations, but few use education in such a way as to build total parish strategy. Many parishes use leadership conferences, but few get and use the variety of outside consultants St. Mark's does.

The parish style modeled here is an incorporative style. It is a style that brings in outside help as standard procedure, not as a last-ditch way to survive a crisis. St. Mark's, in spite of its intense involvement in its own inner life and identity, is a parish uniquely open to the use of resources available in its religious and secular environment.

(By the way, Congress chose not to use St. Mark's land for the Library of Congress. Perhaps some of those balloons got to the right place.)

E. L. D.   with   C. A. H.

6

LEARNINGS ABOUT PARISH LIFE

GENERALIZATIONS FROM THE FOUR STORIES

We have long been aware that individuals run into all kinds of personal problems that block them from living at their full potential. As Christians, we are accustomed to stories of Jesus' good news setting individuals free from such personal bondages.

Similarly, congregations get locked into corporate hang-ups that are just as debilitating, just as frustrating, and just as wasteful of human energy. Instead of healing some of the individuals' hurts, instead of being a force that releases people from their traps, the congregation can even become an obstacle to the person seeking release from his or her personal traps. Such congregations can hurt, not help. They become part of the problem, not the solution.

Just as individuals become captives of forces that lead to unproductive patterns of life, so congregations can become trapped in hurtful, destructive patterns. The bondage of the individual is mirrored in the bondage of the congregation.

Just as individuals long for freedom, so congregations desperately want to be free for their exciting, challenging work of nurture and witness. Captives of their many unfreedoms, congregations seek the release that Jesus' good news is all about.

So it is that congregations have gospel stories, stories of freedom, to tell. Four stories have been told here—stories of ways that four individual congregations found some new freedom. Each of these stories is different. Each reflects the pressures of a particular history, the uniqueness of a particular group of people, and the combination of a special set of circumstances and events. Each found its own special kind of freedom—freedom from *its* particular captivities that kept it from its work of ministry.

These stories are gospel stories. In each of them, a congregation moved from some areas of captivity to some areas of greater freedom. None has solved all its problems. All have found that solving some problems leads to new problems, but that those new problems are often more challenging, more in line with the tasks the congregation wants to do. The congregations have also discovered that their new areas of freedom give them greater strength and resourcefulness in dealing with the new issues that arise.

All of these four congregations moved toward greater freedom for the individual member. The members of First United Presbyterian Church were freed from one-way, pulpit-to-pew communication and freed for a deeper, more supportive and nourishing life of community with one another. Members of all four churches became free from some of their isolation from each other and free to contribute more of their individuality to common parish goals. Particularly at St. Michael's, people were liberated from those barriers that had made worship a cause of anger and recrimination—freed for an unusually deep level of personal communication through acts of worship and freed for expressing their particular identity as a group of God's people in Adelphi. St. Mark's found unusual freedom from routine Christian education—freedom for exciting, involving learning in which the Scriptures came vividly to life. Trustees at St. Bartholomew's discovered some freedom from communications blocks—freedom for a new kind of honesty with one another that made for more effective work.

In short, major movements were made in the area of supporting and strengthening freedom for the person. These four congregations found greater ability to do the nurturing work of ministry.

In the story of each congregation, I can begin to see evidence of conspicuous attention to outward witness where there was little before. Having deepened the work of nurture, each of these congregations is beginning to make greater corporate attempts to address itself to the community it inhabits.

St. Mark's witness in the community has been going on for a long time. Its most recent decisions about investing a portion of its funds for ministry in community needs are dramatic decisions, but they build on a tradition of outside involvement which goes back to its drama group in the 1950s. St. Bartholomew's is far from finished wrestling with the meaning of evangelism and outreach, but the impetus for the wrestling comes from its corporate concern for witness in and to its community. The signs of corporate concern for witness are less sure at First Church in Aberdeen, perhaps because Irwin made the strategic decision that nurture needed most immediate priority; also, perhaps, because the congregation was not ready to make such steps during an interim period. The concern for witness at St. Michael's has been clearly expressed by the commitment of leadership and funds to the community development program of the

Silver Spring Group Ministry. In addition, its Youth and
Adult Committee is well along in its plans to share its learnings with other congregations.

What remains hard to identify is the other aspect of witness—the change in the way *individuals* witness outside
their congregation as a result of the changes in the congregation. A number of individuals have made comments about
how their own witness has been affected by the changes
going on in their congregation, but it is hard to measure this
with any accuracy or even make very helpful generalizations about it. Clearly it is happening, and that is about all
that can be said. One vestryman at St. Michael's reports, for
example, that at his work he is getting called on for help because of his life at St. Michael's. He says, "Sometimes when
problems come along at work, somebody will turn to me
and say, 'For this one, you'll have to turn your collar
around!'"

Each congregation is moving in its own characteristic
way, and each will probably continue to manifest a quite
distinctive approach to witness—one emphasizing good
works in the community, another moving toward activistic
social witness, and another building outreach through religious proclamation. Each of these congregations is moving
toward that form of witness which is authentically its own,
and each is also moving toward that balance of corporate
witness and individual witness which fits its life.

There is a relationship between the nurture going on in a
congregation and the witness it produces. It is clear that little witness happens if the needs of individual lives are not
being met at some depth in the congregation. People who
do not find some freedom from their personal fears, anx-
ieties, and hang-ups generally do not seem to be able to be
free for outgoing witness.

SPECIFIC LEARNINGS
ABOUT CONGREGATIONS

1. Congregations Can Change

What began as my hope and commitment I can now assert against a background of information gathered in action-research. The life of the parish does not have to be something that just happens. Purposeful people can determine much about the direction of the congregation's life. Instead of being trapped in unproductive ways of living, it is possible to make significant headway against the barriers to freedom that get built into our parish life. That which is unrewarding and depressing in congregational life can be changed. There are directions to go and ways to get started. I am painfully aware of large gaps in our knowledge about this process, but I am optimistic about our being able to close some of those gaps. The four stories in this book tell how four congregations took responsibility for the life of their churches, bringing new life to themselves corporately and individually.

This may be the most important thing I can say out of PTP's research. There *is* hope for congregations! There *is* balm in Gilead! Much more freedom is possible.

2. Congregations Have History

It seems strange, but I find few congregations that seem to have a sense of their own history. That lack of a sense of history means they have little sense of where they have been, where they are, or where they are going. Little wonder that they have difficulty *getting* anywhere!

The lives of such ahistorical congregations are episodic.

Events follow one another, but are basically unrelated to each other. Things are always being started over from scratch. What is learned by hard experience by one board or committee has to be learned all over again by the next. Although many congregations build programs around liturgical calendars, each year remains unrelated to previous ones or to the one coming up.

Communications to denominational headquarters reflect this lack of a sense of history. Year-end reports detail statistical information, but the forms do not even ask what *happened*. Although the statistical data may touch the history, it is at least twice removed from how people actually did their work of ministry. Bishops and superintendents of congregations then have to discharge their duties of supervision without really knowing much about what happened and what is happening—knowing only what is rumored through the grape vines that operate at clergy conferences.

Lack of a sense of history is a major source of the trapped feeling people get in congregations. Congregations which do not know their history are in bondage to the whim of the moment. They have no anchor in their own traditions and experience, and they are closed off from a perspective that would let them see where they are in order to make responsible choices about where they want to go.

I believe it is essential for a congregation that wants to develop to put its life in historical perspective. This permits some freedom to try new things, yes; but far more importantly, it makes a new kind of living possible. Knowing one's history means experiencing how God is drawing us out of the past, how he gives us a present moment in which to make choices, and how he both calls us toward the future and awaits us there. That is precisely what it means to be the People of God.

The stories in this book describe four congregations and how they found new freedom by putting their lives into historical perspective. The focus of the stories is just as much on the relationship between the events as it is upon the events themselves. The historical process is the way one event leads to another, either as an attempt to build on previous success or as an attempt to overcome an earlier failure. Each moment's decision or action thus begins to be seen as a step to be evaluated in terms of how well it helps the congregation move toward where it wants to be and how well it builds upon what the congregation has discovered itself to be.

First Church came to understand that it could not have gone on to a covenant with a new pastor without coming to terms with the ways it had for making ministers feel "high, dry, lonesome, and frustrated." By seeing what First Church had done in the past, the congregation was freed for a more constructive relationship with a new pastor. Without that insight into their history, the congregation would have been more likely to repeat its mistakes.

St. Michael's regularly allotted time at vestry meetings, parish meetings, and services to review its history. In the process of thus looking at where they had been and where they wanted to go, St. Michael's members developed an intense sense of identity and were freed for purposeful action.

St. Mark's was convinced that its architectural changes needed to be made in a way that was responsible to its own past, to "those who, to the best of their knowledge and commitment, have sheltered us and given us St. Mark's." The experience of making those changes was seen as important to St. Mark's parishioners in their "now" by pushing them to a clearer sense of their identity, but they were also clear that they wanted to make the building flexible for the use of future generations.

In each of these cases, a sense of history brought freedom. I believe that a sense of parish history is an important, if not an essential, ingredient of parish freedom.

3. Congregations Are Unique

No two congregations are alike. This has very practical implications. Overlooking congregational uniqueness can block parish life in important ways. Parishes often seem to think that they should have a program like the one that seems so successful in the next-door parish. A lot of time gets put into trying to copy successful programs developed elsewhere, and rarely do the results justify the effort.

Out of the PTP research, I am becoming more convinced that the uniqueness of a congregation is its most important asset. I am more and more convinced that any congregation of Christians can carry out its own distinctive ministry with success and integrity, no matter how large or small the congregation may be. Many congregations (particularly small "mission" congregations) are badly hurt by the uniform standards by which their denominational structures judge them. Those standards always concern numbers of people and amounts of money, *not quality and integrity of ministry.* As a result, many congregations in areas of declining population are condemned to "failure" year after year—they simply cannot measure up by the statistical yardsticks. The toll this takes in the lives of the people of the congregations is great enough, but it also tends to keep their attention diverted from the areas of ministry that *are* authentic for their congregation. Because of the irrelevant goals writ in the stone of canon law, scores of fine small congregations never even get the idea that they do have resources for a full and valid life of ministry.

Parish development is a movement that attempts to help congregations develop what they have, deal with the issues that are real for them, and get on with doing the ministry they can do.

In the four stories of parish development we see congregations developing and celebrating their own uniqueness—a uniqueness derived from the special people in that congregation, the special set of worlds those people inhabit, the special set of resources, hopes, convictions, histories, and (yes!) prejudices those people hold.

St. Mark's has a gift for facing life with the utmost honesty, dealing directly with the deepest and most painful experiences people ever meet. The people of First Church have come a long way in learning to share their individual lives with one another—knowing, supporting, communicating with, and caring about one another. St. Michael's has a healthy pride in the way its worship distinctively reflects its corporate personality.

This uniqueness needs to be strengthened and encouraged by those who have the care of the churches. Practically, this means that regional and national church leaders and their staffs need to concentrate on ministering to parishes in ways that encourage growth and support diversity rather than on providing unified program resources or answers.

4. Congregations Are Corporate, Interpersonal Systems

There are two ways of looking at a congregation: one is in terms of its theological meaning and the other is in terms of its life as an organization of human beings. Both are valid. Every congregation needs a healthy attention to both.

The former dimension is important to every congregation, and is reflected in a number of biblical images—the Body of Christ, the Vine and the Vineyard, the People of God, and many others. It is from this theological perspective that sermons and study groups most often consider the life of the Church.

The latter dimension is often neglected by congregations, but is an equally valid way of looking at the life of the parish. It is my conviction that congregations which do neglect this dimension pay a heavy price. Much of the life of the congregation is determined by things that are hard to define—the way people relate to one another, the way information is communicated, the patterns of behavior that are accepted, the way decisions are made and carried out.

I believe that these things have more power than we give them credit for. They do more to determine the character of the congregation than the theology of the sermons or the churchmanship of the laity. Indeed, the deepest beliefs of the members of a congregation can be blocked by the way the congregation acts.

At St. Mark's there was a genuine desire to accept Jim Adams as the new minister, but the congregation could not do so until the people had dealt with the feelings of desertion and grief brought on by their former minister's departure.

Session members in Aberdeen *wanted* to work for First Church, but unclear goals, stiff formality, unresolved conflict, and an atmosphere that made it impossible for them to be *people* to each other made them say, "I was never so glad as when I got off the Session." St. Bartholomew's genuinely wanted everyone to have an opportunity to feel included, but its organizational life was inadequate to permit people to make contributions that made any difference.

It is hard for a parish to witness to the ultimate importance of each person's life when no one knows anyone else's
name. It is hard to communicate the importance of what
people do if, when jobs are handed out, nobody ever checks
up to see if the jobs are done. It is hard to talk of the priesthood of all believers when it is obvious that all the important decisions are made for the congregation by a small
informal committee that "knows what is best." It is hard to
be an open, loving community when no opportunities are
made for people to meet one another face-to-face. It is hard
to welcome new members if they are never helped to get involved in the life of the parish.

A parish that is unaware of the corporate dimension of its
life is likely to get trapped in unproductive patterns of life.

A parish that is aware of this dimension can use its knowledge to build and support new freedom. These informal patterns of relationship can hinder a congregation's life, but
patterns can be built that open doors for individuals and the
group. The patterns can be just as strong in support of ministry as they can be in frustrating ministry.

Members of the Board of Trustees at St. Bartholomew's
found that their inability to speak clearly and directly to one
another about how they honestly felt led them into confused
and uncertain decisions and kept them from accomplishing
much. On the other hand, as they built better communication between each other, their new pattern helped them toward their goals. At St. Michael's, an unwillingness to listen
to one another when sharp differences arose over worship
led to a split and polarized the congregation. Later, after experience in dealing with other conflicts, they discovered
that when conflict *did* arise, careful listening could lead to a
much deeper understanding of each other and a more exciting life together.

I think we are only beginning to understand this dimension of congregational life. I am confident that much more can be learned, and I believe those learnings will open more doors for productivity and increased effectiveness of congregations.

Where the corporate, interpersonal, and systemic dimensions of congregational life are taken seriously, new freedom occurs.

LEARNINGS ABOUT THE PROCESS OF CHANGE IN CONGREGATIONS

1. Third-Party Consultation Can Increase the Rate and Effectiveness of Change in a Congregation

The adviser/consultant who enters a congregation brings an objectivity that in itself is a major contribution. He or she is able to see things that members of the congregation cannot see—that is, not until the consultant asks the right questions. I believe that one of the best gifts adviser/consultants bring is what I call their "innocent ignorance." Because the adviser/consultants are innocent and unrelated to the parish's past history, the congregation is willing to permit them to ask questions out of their ignorance—questions often bringing out in the open issues that had been held in a conspiracy of silence. The adviser/consultant's question: "Why is it that the Finance Committee never makes a report to the board?" can well open up issues that *must* be dealt with. Perhaps that committee always acts in secret and other board members are resentful of it; perhaps the committee is . angry because it had no control over last year's building fund campaign; perhaps no one ever happened to think of the relationship between finances and the work of the

board. The point is that the board will generally accept such
a question from an outsider and begin to deal with the issues
that come to the surface. An "insider" would know that it is
a "no-no" question, one that might embarrass a member of
the Finance Committee. The adviser/consultant's innocent ignorance helps a congregation gain access to their
own important issues.

There are many kinds of consultants. The chapter on St.
Mark's shows that parish's unusual ability to orchestrate the
use of many kinds of consultants—psychiatric, organization
development, architectural, and planning, among others.
My own experience leads me to feel that the best kinds of
consultants are those (by whatever name they are called)
who do not come in to develop answers *for* the congregation, but who come in to help the parish discover its own
questions and answers and help the congregation gain the
ability to put those answers into action. Certain skills are essential—some skill in understanding organizational life,
some skill in helping people overcome blocks to their own
communication, some skill in helping people learn from
their experience and practice new behavior. Consultants
who overwhelm congregations with their "expertise" are
likely to encourage unhealthy dependence and are generally
to be avoided.

A major concern of any consultant will be to broaden the
base of decision-making, bringing as many members of the
congregation as possible into the role of "owner" rather
than "observer" of parish life. That is why the consultants
led St. Mark's, St. Bartholomew's, and St. Michael's to have
parishwide sessions to gather information as a basis for planning. That is why Irwin led a series of Lenten sessions for a
broad segment of the congregation to mull over information

about the life of the congregation in preparation for beginning to do something about it.

As this broadening of the base of decision-making occurs,
the congregation often finds that people who were thought
of as passive wallflowers have significant contributions they
want to and will make. Often these people are quiet because they found no opportunities to get in on the action.
Often they have been rejected because they were seen as
negative and critical. Part of their contribution may well
start out as criticism. Any parish that prepares to move toward development must expect that new voices will be
heard, that new criticisms will come to light, and that some
comfortable things will be changed.

Because these dynamics are not always easy or comfortable, the objectivity of the consultant can be a great asset in
guiding the congregation through its growing pains.

At the point in the process at Aberdeen when Keith Irwin
picked up the new shoe to illustrate his role as a consultant,
he said to the people, "Some things I'll be doing will be new
and different. Perhaps at times the new things may cause a
bit of pain—like this shoe!"

A clear word of caution is in order. The third-party role is
not always effective. There are cases in which the chemistry
of the consultant and that of the congregation or the clergyman simply do not mix. Sometimes the consultant gets
trapped into becoming part of the congregation, losing his
or her objectivity and taking sides. Sometimes a clergyman
or a board backs away from the risks of responsibility. There
have been times in the PTP experimentation when outside
supervision helped sort out what was happening and got the
consultation back on track. There have been other times
when the method simply did not work, and no amount of

effort seemed to get things back on the track. There are no guarantees.

Consultants, in this book and in the work of Project Test Pattern, function to help the congregation define its own life and its own goals, and to remove the blocks that act as barriers. The use of the third-party consultant increases the speed and effectiveness with which a congregation begins to use its own resources and manages its own process of change.

2. Covenant/Contract Relationships Help

I have found that people in congregations are not sure what to expect from each other. The clergyman is often at the center of this lack of clarity, and he is often the chief victim. Each member of the congregation has his or her unspoken expectations of what the minister will be and do. The minister himself is often trapped by those expectations, not knowing clearly what they are, unable to fulfill some and unwilling to fulfill others. Likewise, in parish organizations people are assigned tasks but have very unclear understandings of how to get help, to whom to report, or when the job assignment is over. Personal evaluation goes on behind people's backs, but rarely face-to-face. (How many comments about poor sermons there are, and how little help there is to make the preaching and the listening more satisfying to both the congregation and the preacher!)

All too often the result is that it does not really seem to matter if committee members follow through or not. Other results are low morale, lack of trust, inability to get even simple tasks done, low sense of accomplishment, and general frustration.

Experience in the PTP network leads me to believe that

the clear contractual agreements between consultant and congregation are quite freeing in this very area of expectations. By stating clearly what will be done and what will not be done, and by specifying a schedule for getting a task done, the consultant and the congregation find themselves free to get on with their task. The congregation is able to hold the consultant accountable for what he or she agreed to do. Likewise, the consultant can hold the congregation accountable for what it agreed to do in their relationship. If, as is described in (1) above, the relationship between the parish and the consultant is not producing satisfying results, there must be a clear way for either party to say so and terminate the relationship.

In Aberdeen, Irwin and the Session clearly agreed to a set of priorities for his work, which was particularly important since he had only a limited time. That contract was frequently referred to during his seven months in Aberdeen, and it supported him and the Session in doing high-priority work, not just "baby-sitting" the congregation during the interim.

There are people who find the word "contract" harsh and inappropriate for life in the Church. Although I have no objection to this word, I do believe the word "covenant" expresses more of what I mean—a clear agreement which involves commitment to a relationship in which the parties are accountable to each other for their faithfulness.

It is clear to me that a barrier to congregational freedom is this lack of clarity about responsibilities. Wider use of contracts or covenants between clergy and their lay boards is likely to lead to increased freedom for getting tasks done. The principle could even be helpful in such prosaic matters as committee assignments.

3. The Clergyman Is a Key to Change in the Congregation

When a congregation undergoes change, the clergyman experiences increased anxiety and feelings of stress. He, more than others in the congregation, finds change threatening as well as exciting and fulfilling.

A particular problem in most congregations is that both the clergyman and the members tend to look to the minister as a *source* of support, not as a *recipient* of support. Not much thought is given to seeing that his emotional needs are met, and often he has difficulty admitting his needs or accepting genuine support even when it is available.

What is a problem in ordinary times can become a crisis when the tension and stress of congregational change is added to the picture. Congregations seem often to be unaware of this dynamic and unable to give adequate personal support.

During the process of change outlined in these stories, the consultant can help provide some of this support, but those who have responsibility for churches in the area (bishops, superintendents, and others) are also potential resources.

The long-term answer, of course, is to build congregations whose ability to provide personal support is shown by lay members and clergymen who are sensitive to moments of intense stress.

The clergyman's willingness to accept risk is essential if the congregation is to enter a process of development and to work with him in developing a collaborative approach to their joint ministry. The change that appears to be a matter of academic interest to some members of a congregation may involve the deepest level of a clergyman's personal life. Without his willingness to take risks, it is unlikely that much is going to happen.

Jim Adams had to be willing to risk criticism of his sermons before he was able to help the St. Mark's congregation discover a problem that was blocking its life. Keith Irwin's willingness to try a demanding double role as a pastor and a consultant involved him in personal risk, but it helped First Church grow in its ability to relate to pastors. Ron Albaugh's growth into a strong, decisive leader at St. Michael's required him to take difficult and risky steps of professional evaluation and personal growth. Dick Gilchrist found that the changes needed at St. Bartholomew's required him to dare to try new, more direct ways of stating his feelings.

The strength these four men showed is not something that can be taken for granted. There are excellent parish ministers who would find such steps impossible. Some clergy seem to come by the ability to take risks easily, but for most the ability comes only when they live in a strength-giving, supportive community. Living in such a supportive community can help free the minister to accept the risks of leadership—the kind of leadership that is such an important key to continuing development of the congregation.

4. Support Systems Are Important

Throughout our work in parishes, we kept running into the need people and groups have for a kind of back-up from others. Sometimes this is just emotional support during a particularly trying time, sometimes it is technical help in working out a solution, sometimes it is providing a perspective from the outside.

The experience in Aberdeen was particularly illustrative of several levels of this need for support. Keith Irwin and I developed a very close relationship, in which I was free to question and criticize what he was doing, in which I provided some emotional support and encouragement when he was down. We both found this to be a warm and strong relationship, but the point is that he found his work more effective because of it.

At another level, the presbytery, by setting up an Administrative Commission for First Church, gave support to the entire congregation in working toward needed changes. Although administrative commissions can legally act in an almost arbitrary way, *this* commission saw its task as supporting and encouraging the congregation, always working with and through the Session members. That congregation found a support system that *did* challenge it to deal with a problem, yet did so in a way that encouraged the growth of the congregation's problem-solving ability. At yet another level, the congregation began to provide a base for more personal support for individuals.

In the other three congregations where the consultants worked with the local clergyman, there was the added and important dimension mentioned above of the support the consultants provided for that clergyman during the process of change.

The concept of the support system is important in dealing with congregations. The congregation *is* a support system for its people. Its nurture supports the people individually, in their families, in their work, and in their community. Where the support system is weak, the effectiveness of the witness is weakened. Where the support system is strong or growing stronger, there is almost immediate impact in the lives of individuals.

The congregation *needs* a support system. In the cases we considered, the four congregations were supported directly by outside forces. St. Michael's change process was made possible by the fact that the Diocese of Washington had a

consultant on its staff trained to help parishes. St. Bartholomew's work was made possible by a collaboration of forces
from the Diocese of Alabama and the national resources of
the Episcopal Church. What happened at Aberdeen was
supported not only by the presbytery, but by the Mid-Atlan-
tic Training Committee, an ecumenical coalition that
trained Keith Irwin, and by cooperation between the Division of Evangelism of the United Presbyterian Church and
Project Test Pattern. What happened at St. Mark's was supported by the Diocese of Washington, but also by the mix of
community resources and trained people that St. Mark's
called upon.

In this connection, something needs to be said about the
difficulty regional church bodies find in providing a support
system for parishes. For a long time the local congregations
have operated as submissive and obedient children, accepting the answers worked out for them in their regional or national offices. The rebellion of many congregations against
those answers is at least partly a healthy demand for the
freedom of self-determination. As such, it is an expression of
freedom and of growing maturity, although it often has the
feel of adolescent rebellion against authority. The changes
involved in this rebellion are profound both for the congregation and for its regional church support system.

This increasing freedom represents frightening new responsibility for the congregation. If the work of the local
congregation continues to be anemic and irrelevant, the
bishop is no longer to blame. If integrity of mission and ministry is to be developed, it must be developed by the people
involved in the local parish, not in far-off national offices.
The congregation is now free for its unique ministry and
mission. It will be judged by the quality of the fruit it produces. The scapegoats are gone.

Regional leaders and bishops are challenged by this concept of a support system, since it is in opposition to past patterns of their relationship to their congregations. In past patterns congregations were valued for their willingness to support diocesan or national policy. In the pattern I am describing, diocesan and national organizations or officers are valued for their ability to support and encourage the initiative of the local congregations. At the moment parishes and bishops are caught in the middle of this shift. It is just as difficult for congregations to learn to be independent as it is for bishops to learn to live with maturing, sometimes rebellious congregations. Bishops and their staffs have new skills to learn for this enabling ministry, but never have parishes needed a skillful pastoral support system more than now.

5. *Valuable Learnings Can Come from Failure*

Congregations often seem unable to celebrate their victories because they are so afraid of failure. They are also afraid to try things because they fear that they will not achieve their goals. The four congregations we described here found that what seemed to be a failure could become a moment of growth if they were prepared to look carefully at what had happened, learn from it, and go on to the next steps. Indeed, St. Michael's has its own symbol, "the morning after," to describe the time when reflection on past action can lead to new directions. The symbol came from a morning session spent reflecting on the previous night's debacle of miscommunication and misunderstanding.

I cannot leave this point without stating quite clearly that I found this to be true in the life of Project Test Pattern as well as in the life of congregations. The deployment of consultants to congregations is far from an exact science, and I

can identify a number of significant mistakes that I made,
that consultants made, that we made in conjunction, and
that happened without my quite knowing how they happened:

. . . Consultants are sent into a congregation with one
idea of what they have been asked to do; the congregation
has meanwhile been prepared for a totally different approach; so, the two waste a day in mystified miscommunication.

. . . Consultants are invited into a congregation and start
to go to work, not knowing that the vestry that invited them
in has been replaced by a new vestry that knows nothing
about what the consultants are doing.

. . . I get a report from a consultant team in which they
ask for help with a difficult problem, but I do not recognize
their need until too late.

The list is not endless, but it is long enough to make the
point that consultations do not always work. Even where
they do not work, there is the possibility of learning a considerable amount by digging into what actually happened.
In each of these cases we arranged field trips to find out
from the consultants and the congregation what had actually happened; and we tried to turn what we learned into
better ways of helping other congregations and training
other consultants.

The fact that valuable learnings can come from failure
does not rob failure of its pain. The clergyman can get hurt,
the congregation can get hurt, the consultants can get hurt.
But clergymen and congregations are getting hurt already
by what happens now. People are getting left like hit-and-
run victims behind the wheels of our well-run vestry meetings and congregational projects, and nobody ever looks

back to pick them up or to find out why they have been run down.

A congregation that will examine its experience closely will have the possibility of turning some of its pain into growing pains. Accepting the dimension of hurt that is happening will make possible learning and growth and also open the doors for appreciation of the triumphant moments of congregational life.

WORSHIP: EXPRESSION AND SOURCE OF THE CONGREGATION'S LIFE

The role of worship in a congregation's life and in its process of change deserves special mention.

It is clear from what I have seen in congregations that worship is not "just another" activity. It has peculiar meanings and power in defining the identity of the congregation and the people who make it up. Its role in a congregation is analogous to the role of sex in marriage—at one and the same time it expresses and reaffirms the common life and it *also* generates new possibilities. It celebrates what *is*, but also it opens doors for better things.

Worship has a particularly rich relationship to a congregation's self-awareness and sense of identity. It dramatizes, at its best, that which the congregation sees to be most authentic about its life. It gives that identity and authenticity symbolic and dramatic form. That very form then becomes a new point of departure for discovering and symbolizing new aspects of the corporate identity. The openness that people at First Church began to find in small groups was reinforced when they met on Sunday mornings, not only by the content and style of the preaching but by the way the preacher began to give opportunities for the people to give face-to-face reactions. What was formal and impersonal moved toward deeply personal acts of worship in which the congregation was able to give the warm support that poured out toward the graduating high school seniors. St. Mark's Whitsunday service was characteristic of its liturgical life. The service, planned in St. Mark's own inimitable celebrative style, was adapted on the spot to reflect the people's concern that the building they loved might be destroyed. Then that concern was immediately turned into action to do something about the threat to their life. At St. Michael's the whole process of change was integrally related to worship. Worship was the most difficult and divisive issue, but it gradually became the clear center of the congregation's identity—an identity that insists upon the validity and importance of each person's deep individual needs.

Congregations in general vastly underrate the power of their worship. The power is related to the intensity of each individual's investment in the meanings and symbols of his or her faith and the absolutely incalculable power of those meanings and symbols as they are lifted up in the congregation's worship. My impression is that the expression of a congregation's life through its worship has much greater power over personal and corporate identity than has ever been suspected. The corporate symbol has much more power than the sum of the individuals' symbols. Our experience has been that the consultant's objectivity and skill are particularly useful in dealing with these powerful personal dynamics.

My own concern, based upon what has been discovered in congregations, is that those who make national or regional policy on liturgical matters might take this power much more seriously as liturgical change is planned. Providing better forms for worship is an academic issue; getting them through conventions is a political matter. Changing those forms in a local congregation touches the very core of a people's being. More needs to be known about these dynamics. *Much* more help needs to be given to congregations to understand and deal with the power of the dynamics of worship.

PARISH RENEWAL: A PROCESS, NOT A PROGRAM

It is my experience that the renewal of the parish is a complex process, not an event or a program. The breakthrough to freedom is not an event that happens and then is accomplished forever. It is a long, arduous process that requires the best energies and talents that men and women have to give to the task.

This learning goes contrary to an assumption that seems to lie at the heart of many congregations—the assumption that some new idea, some new program, some new bolt from the blue will renew the parish. In periods of crisis in a congregation this assumption often appears as the idea that firing one minister and hiring another will solve the congregation's problems. I have seen extraordinary and unforeseen things happen that bring life to people in a congregation, but my experience is that those unexpected appearances of grace seem to happen more often where people are hard at work using their skills and insights to build better congregations. More than that—I find that any congregation that does not pay attention to its ongoing life process is like the poor soil of Jesus' parable, lacking the depth and sustenance to let things grow. Quite a few imaginative programs bring momentary excitement or revival to a congregation, but in most cases the enthusiasm soon gives way to new frustra-

tion. It takes hard, dedicated work to build congregations
that can *use* programs for sustained growing.

The best analogies we have for the process of parish renewal are analogies of growth. A great marriage is not an
event: it is a lifelong process by which two people become
ever more distinct, yet ever more united. In the course of a
great marriage there are moments of division and bitterness
and anger. There are also moments when it all seems hollow
and useless. Yet the mark of a great marriage is that those
moments are overcome. As these blocks to communication
occur, they are broken through to another and deeper level
of life. Probably some of those blocks are never removed.
The point of the marriage is not any particular event in it,
not even the moments of happiness and celebration. The
point is that the great moments are celebrated and the terrible moments are accepted and dealt with. Each successive
moment becomes a step toward the next movement of
growth.

Parish renewal is like that. It is not one breakthrough
from captivity; it is a continuing process by which the people of a congregation move through their common life meeting obstacles and celebrating victories, constantly deepening the effectiveness of their ministry. The process can be
seen in the years of tenacious work we have described at St.
Mark's, but also in the way St. Michael's tackled one problem, then another, and another, gradually building the ability to solve the more difficult problems which were blocking
the people from their ministry and from one another. It can
also be seen in the way First Church gradually, over a
seven-month period, moved from a competitive, every-man-
for-himself concept of ministry, to a position in which its
people began to see themselves as a ministering team and

began to look for a new pastor who could lead them as a team, not one who would do it all himself.

I suspect that we have only begun to imagine what can be learned about congregations. There is so much unexplored territory. I only wonder that so few of the churches' resources have been used in such exploration. I wonder that theological faculties and seminaries focus so little of their interest, energy, or research effort on the local unit of ministry, the congregation.

The little bit that we have begun to uncover is already proving to be most useful in helping parishes with their process of development. Using what we have discovered is also helping us begin to locate more promising areas for exploration and to design better methods of research.

For over a century now, the churches have been using with great profit a variety of new skills in biblical research and inquiry, historical criticism and form criticism. These skills have become essential tools in interpreting the Christian message today. This book describes some newer God-given skills of analysis and communication, planning and decision-making, evaluation and management, which are making possible important breakthroughs to new effectiveness for the ministering community, the congregation.

I have indicated how some of these skills were used in four specific situations. Another part of the story might be how the tools the consultants used were developed and shared. Keith Irwin used a tool early in his work that had been developed in northern Michigan by other PTP consultants. Jim Anderson used a method at St. Michael's that he adapted from a design he discovered in Maine. Harry Pritchett and Martha Adams used some ideas that had first been tested in Maryland. Some of those methods have become obsolete as we have discovered more effective ones. Some of the tools we now use will be looked at in a few years as stone age tools. At the moment, however, they are the best we have, and we can see that they can help improve the quality of parish life.

Although these learnings represent only the tip of the iceberg, it is clear that a major resource in closing the gap between performance and potential in the congregation lies in the talents and skills of ordinary people who will commit themselves to the purposeful change of their congregations.

7

THE CHRISTIAN GOSPEL AND
THE PARISH CHURCH

THE GOSPEL OF FREEDOM

We have told the story of four congregations as they moved toward greater freedom and looked at some learnings from their experience. Now I need to say why I think what has happened in those places is of extraordinary importance. This means trying to state an operational kind of theology—a theology that talks about God's work in relation to the intentions and actions of men. The good news of God is communicated as a story of people in relationship to each other and to God. It is a story of people discovering the power to be more truly human, people being freed from all kinds of bondages, people helping each other become free, people discovering a kind of freedom that seems to come from the heights and depths of existence. The Bible is not a book of philosophy or even of theology. It is an anthology of freedom stories.

There are stories being added to that anthology daily. The Bible tells of God's good news of freedom—the freedom of a Saul for becoming Paul the Apostle, the freedom of poor, vacillating Peter for becoming a spiritual rock. It is just that

117

kind of freedom that happened a few years ago when a tired black woman sat down on a city bus in Montgomery, and it is the kind of freedom a high school boy in Aberdeen was talking about when he told me: "I'm so open now it scares me." The story of Ron Albaugh's discovery of himself as a strong and effective leader is a story of freedom—a modern gospel story.

Our stories of congregations grappling with issues of freedom point out how the quality of the corporate life has direct impact upon the lives of individuals. Members of those four congregations did not intend to hurt each other or misunderstand each other, and yet the way they lived together corporately made them do the things they did not want to do and to leave undone the things they wanted to do.

In every person and in every institution there are powerful enemies to freedom. Paul calls the corporate adversaries such as we have seen operating in these four churches "principalities and powers." They are strange forces that we do not understand, perhaps generated in every person's instinct to protect and preserve himself and his own freedom even when it costs others their freedom. Whatever these forces are and wherever they come from, they are very real in our institutions and in our congregations. There is some wisdom in the scriptural personification of these forces as "the Adversary," or Satan. I am beginning to think that we would do well to have a more healthy respect for this power and to mobilize all the resources we can to defeat "his" purposes. The principle of operation I have drawn from this insight is that I no longer expect freedom to come without a fight.

Breakthrough to freedom at the corporate level of life is just as much a gospel story as it is for the individual. When First Church members gathered around their high school seniors, they experienced a breakthrough in corporate life that was a dramatic and important expression of the gospel. There are some parallels between what happened that day in South Dakota and what happened nearly two thousand years ago in Antioch when the members of another local congregation gathered around Paul and Silas as they commenced their vocations as missionaries.

THE RESPONDING COMMUNITY

The Church is not a community that "owns" or "dispenses" this good news. The freedom comes from God and appears at unpredictable times and places, sometimes among the most unlikely people. The mark of God's presence is the appearance of freedom, whether it be the freedom of an individual who breaks out from ignorance or prejudice, that of a person who actualizes a new capacity for entering into a relationship with another, that of a person breaking out of political or social bondage, that of a person experiencing freedom from sickness or guilt or depression. This gospel is not contained by any institution. This gospel runs free. The whole world is shot through with it.

From the earliest accounts in the New Testament, the Church has seen itself as a fellowship of people who are called to act in response to God's initiative. The history of the Church is full of instances in which it has been unfaithful in responding and of times when the principalities and powers seemed to overcome the power of God's freedom. It is always reassuring to know that God has ways of bringing the power of his gospel to his people even when they seem hopelessly bound up in unfreedom. When American piety tried to build a purely private religion, God raised up a mighty agent of social change and social freedom—Martin

Luther King. When the churches built higher and higher walls of mistrust and suspicion between each other, God raised up a disarming, simple old man of peasant stock who changed the world with his talk of reconciliation—Pope John XXIII. When St. Michael's people became polarized, half favoring traditional and half innovative worship, there was raised up a Worship Task Force of ordinary Christians who were finally able to hear the language of each other's hearts and build a worship life for all.

As a community that responds to God's work of freedom, the Church has seen its task as a double one. The metaphors that have been used for two thousand years reflect the two dimensions of the work—the gathering and the scattering, the journey inward and the journey outward, the coming in and the going out. Basically, the inward movement is the work of the Church's nurture of her own people, building them up in faith. The outward movement is the living out of the great commandment of Jesus that the Church go to all people proclaiming his good news. It is the work of witnessing by word and action to the works of freedom that God is doing in his world for his people, whether they acknowledge his lordship or not.

TASKS OF THE RESPONDING COMMUNITY: NURTURE

"Build each other up in the faith" was a theme in many of Paul's letters to churches and individuals. Ever since his time this theme has been an important concern for those in local congregations. Certainly it was a major concern of the four parishes described in this book. Each, in its own way, was concerned with finding ways for its members to reach their potential in faith. Since biblical times there have been three major sources of nurture: the life of the community itself, the content and meaning of the Scriptures, and the special holy actions which express and build up the character of the community's life—those actions that are called sacramental by many Christians.

Remarkable resources are found in any congregation that will use its corporate life as a source of nurture. Talented, committed people who are prepared to care for others are a scarce commodity in our depersonalized society. A sense of community, of belonging, is still easier to find in some rural areas, but even there life patterns are changing. The style of life developed at St. Mark's shows how the life of a congregation can provide power for living in the midst of all the problems of urban life. St. Michael's young people and adults broke new ground for each other when they discovered how much they needed from each other and how much they had to give. This is the *positive* side of what I have said about powers and principalities: the corporate structures can be powerful deterrents to life, but they can be reshaped to become powerful sustainers and encouragers of the growth of individuals.

The Scriptures are another major source of nurture. Keith Irwin used the Scriptures constantly in ways the Church has come to accept as normal—as the source of preaching. But he used these Scriptures in a way that spoke to what the people of First Church were identifying as their particular difficulties and bondages as a congregation. That traditional use was supported by methods of using Scriptures in small groups and at retreats. Nurture happened.

The actions of the community that are seen as especially holy are often called sacramental, but I am using the term quite broadly. Each of these congregations did experience moments of great nurturing power in the actions that are traditionally seen as sacramental—the agape feast First Church people shared at Blue Cloud Abbey, for example. But other moments occurred that do not fit the traditional concepts of "sacramental," but which were powerfully moving experiences of nurture and growth and of exposure to "the Holy": the grief work of St. Mark's people over the death of Harriet Gregory, the guitar playing and the singing of St. Bartholomew's trustees, the silence St. Michael's people learned to share, the laughter First Church Session members began to enjoy.

These are the resources of every congregation—its life as a community, its Scriptures, its sacramental experiences. These can be powerful resources for the nurture of the people. The forces that keep these resources from being effective are forces which the four congregations described in this book have begun to work to overcome. There are encouraging signs that they are achieving some success.

TASKS OF THE RESPONDING COMMUNITY: WITNESS

The remarkable Old Testament story of Jonah is a dramatic statement about the way God goes about his work of freedom in his own way, outside the orthodox channels. Jonah's reluctant journey to the hated Ninevites was a mission to the "outsider" to proclaim God's good news. Jesus expressed God's concern for the Roman and the Syro-Phoenician as well as the despised Samaritan. The People of God have always found God at work outside their sanctuary walls, no matter how often they tried to pretend that he was under control. As a people responding to his works of freedom, their work has always had the outward thrust, the sense of being sent out. There have been three major modes of this outward movement—prophetic witness, participative witness, and celebrative witness.

Prophetic witness occurs when a Christian or a group of Christians proclaim God's freedom in terms of a specific bondage in the world. Prophetic witness can occur in ringing words that get headlines, in a reasoned argument between two people, or in picket lines. We sometimes lose sight of the prophetic witness implicit in what a congregation can proclaim by the quality of its life together—giving a model of living in which a person is valued for what he is, not for what he has. The four congregations in this book seem to be attempting to build that kind of prophetic witness in their communities, and there are strong signs that at least three of them are producing corporate actions of prophetic witness in relationship to the unfreedom of the community around them. As for words of witness, it is encouraging to note that as much prophecy seems to come from the pew as from the pulpit at St. Mark's and St. Michael's.

Participative witness occurs when the Christian goes to join forces with anybody who is working for freedom. St. Bartholomew's actually found it difficult to carry out its work of nurture because its people were so involved in participative witness in community action groups of one kind or another. St. Mark's people and St. Michael's people worked hard during the Poor People's March on Washington in 1968. Their newer relationships to Capitol Hill community groups and to the Silver Spring Group Ministry are a continuation of that witness.

Celebrative witness ordinarily occurs on Sunday morning when the people bring into their act of worship their concerns about their own or their community's unfreedom or their joy at a new breakthrough to freedom that they have experienced or seen. Each of these congregations has found ways of bringing the outside world into its worship in its own characteristic way. The most dramatic example was the Whitsunday service at St. Mark's, where celebration occurred in a context of a street procession, political involvements, and deep concern for the meanings of the past history of the congregation.

THE DOUBLE TASK OF MINISTRY

Nurture and witness are deeply interrelated. Witness without grounding in nurture quickly becomes social activism that lacks direction and sacrifices people for "the cause." Nurture without witness raises up members of a religious club who seek nothing but their own spiritual comfort. Such Christians are like the fig tree Jesus cursed because it bore no figs.

Congregations themselves have to determine the particular mix of nurture and witness that is appropriate for them, taking into consideration their own resources and the needs of their world. This is a complex task, and congregations need help to do it well.

8

THE PARISH CHURCH:
HOPE FOR TOMORROW

The parish is here to stay. I have no qualms about making this unqualified statement.

Local congregations are exceptionally tough institutions. They have remarkable tenacity, and they survive calamities almost as a matter of routine. They bob to the surface after revolutions, plagues, and counterrevolutions. They exist in atheistic cultures and in highly religious cultures. They live on under persecution, and they live on when pampered and protected—in each case sorely tested by the experience.

The parish arrived on the scene long before there were any scriptures of the New Testament and long before the Church had any formal theologies. The congregations produced the people who wrote the Scriptures and the theologies. Many of those who have proclaimed the death of the congregation have been carried to their final resting place from services held in simple parish churches.

I do not worry about the survival of the local congregation. I do worry about the quality of the parish that survives and what we can do about that. Much of the ineffectiveness that I see in congregations now I hope not to see in parishes of the future—their ineffectiveness in delivering their ministry either to individual people or to the issues of the world.

As I look at parishes today the biblical image of the Exodus becomes more and more relevant. I see Christians living in a kind of bondage in their parishes, estranged from what they want to be for each other and the world. I see people and parishes called to another kind of exodus. It will be like the exodus Moses began, an exodus that began with breaking out to freedom, but which involved thousands of years of continuing to break out of new bondages.

There is widespread fascination with the future today. The fascination is partly excitement and curiosity, and it is partly dread. Those who write about what will be happening to us twenty or forty years from now spend half of their pages exciting us with new ideas and half describing nightmares of technological "efficiency," depersonalization, and demoralization. We know very little with any certainty except that the world will be very different, the issues of life will be very different, and existence will probably be more complex and uncertain.

That strange, unknown land of the future is the destination of our new exodus. As God called Moses toward the Promised Land and as he called Jonah to go to Nineveh, he calls *our* congregations to minister in that unknown, uncharted country of the future, adapting our nurture and witness to whatever life will be like there.

What of parishes in that strange land? It really becomes irrelevant to worry about many of the things congregations concern themselves with today when we think of the ministry they are called to in tomorrow's world. It does not really seem to matter much if future congregations have buildings or not, although I suspect many of them will find buildings useful. It does not really matter very much whether future parishes have full-time clergymen with theological degrees on their staffs, although I suspect that many congregations will find it important to have trained men and women available.

But the people of those congregations will be deeply involved with the Bible, wrestling to understand it in terms of the life-styles of that world. They will confront each other and they will encourage each other in finding the most appropriate ways to witness to Jesus Christ in their world with whatever resources they have. Congregations will welcome diversity—different kinds of people, different points of view, and different ideas will not only be tolerated, they will be encouraged.

The biblical image of Jesus will be very important to them as a picture of what it means to live in freedom as a fully human being. Congregations will be likely to welcome conflict and controversy as the price one must pay to affirm the unique value of each person and his point of view. In those congregations will be some who see faith primarily in terms of a vital personal relationship to Jesus Christ, and there will be others who see faith as inseparable from political and social action. Those congregations will be open and receptive to the world, interacting with what goes on outside the parish as fully as possible. Each will try to find ways of bringing into its membership those who have not found their way into the Church, but each will also deeply respect the integrity of what God does through those who do his works while not knowing his name.

The people in the congregations will make mistakes and get frustrated, but they will move on, learning and trying new ways. Each congregation will work to encourage the maximum possible personal growth for each of its members.

From time to time future congregations will raise up the great men and women of faith who will speak prophetic words that will shake that world of tomorrow.

Regularly, but perhaps not always on Sundays, members of those congregations will gather in some common place. And when they gather they will share their deepest concerns with each other and with God. They will explore the Scriptures and perhaps sing a song or two. Someone will probably preach from the Scriptures. Then they will gather around a table of some kind, and someone will bring a loaf of bread and a bottle of wine. . . .

It is to that far country that our congregations are on their exodus. They will find as Moses did that traveling through the wilderness involves hardships. But they will also find resources along the way. There are many who are ready for the journey. Each person who has lived in a congregation also knows that from time to time there are genuine foretastes of the freedom toward which the journey moves.

The people of St. Mark's and St. Michael's, of First Church and St. Bartholomew's know some of the frustrations of the new exodus, but they have also tasted some of the fruits.

It will be from the congregations of tomorrow's world that the good news of freedom will be proclaimed in the face of bondages we cannot even imagine. It is in the congregations of tomorrow's world that the saints, both ordinary and extraordinary, will be equipped for their ministry. It will be from congregations that the saints will go forth participating in, proclaiming, and celebrating the mighty works of freedom God will be accomplishing.

It is our task to take the great tradition of ministry that has been given us by past generations and to begin in our own time to build parishes for tomorrow.